Edward A. Freeman

WINNING TENNIS
AFTER FORTY

ACCOMPLISHMENTS AND AWARDS OF
JASON MORTON AND RUSSELL SEYMOUR

1977 National Hard Court, Clay Court,
Grass Court, and Indoor Senior Doubles Champions

Ranked Number 1 in Doubles and Numbers 1 and 2
in Singles in the U.S. Forty-five and Over Division

Honored by awards as two of the most
outstanding tennis instructors in the United States

Taught ten national and international champions

Winners of innumerable national and
international major event titles and championships

WINNING TENNIS
AFTER FORTY

Jason Morton and Russell Seymour
with Clyde Burleson

PRENTICE-HALL, INC., Englewood Cliffs, New Jersey

To Edith and Jean,
Two great mixed doubles partners who
have helped more than they will ever know

Winning Tennis After Forty
by Jason Morton, Russell Seymour,
and Clyde Burleson
Printed in the United States of America
Prentice-Hall International, Inc., London
Prentice-Hall of Australia, Pty. Ltd., Sydney
Prentice-Hall of Canada, Ltd., Toronto
Prentice-Hall of India Private Ltd., New Delhi
Prentice-Hall of Japan, Inc., Tokyo
Prentice-Hall of Southeast Asia Pte. Ltd., Singapore
Whitehall Books Limited, Wellington, New Zealand
10 9 8 7 6 5 4 3 2 1

Library of Congress Cataloging in Publication Data
Morton, Jason
    Winning tennis after forty.
    1.   Tennis.   2.   Middle age.   I.   Seymour,
Russell, joint author.
II.   Burleson, Clyde W., joint author.
III.   Title.
GV995.M56   796.34'22   79-19846
ISBN 0-13-961169-X

Contents

HOW TO USE THIS BOOK

This is a book for senior players who have attained a certain level of maturity in life. The information here, or much of it, is of equal value to people who are new to the sport as well as experts. Experience has shown us that newcomers over the age of thirty-five or forty can learn the mental side of tennis as they establish their physical game. In other words, seniors potentially have an edge over younger players in that they are able to see more facets of a problem and deal with a larger number of variables.

Beginners who start in their late thirties have another advantage. They miss the experience of having to unlearn the game they spent years developing in their teens and twenties. Every successful over-forty player who started hitting balls in high school or college has had to go through this. It's a metamorphosis made all the harder by the fact you are not as physically able and not as agile. Since a failing tennis game is often the first tangible sign many people have of their aging, the changing of their style of play may well become associated with acquiescence of advancing age.

By contrast, players who take up the game past their mid-thirties do not have to unlearn previously successful strokes and reactions. They start from a playing base suitable to their years. Because their physical side is not as high as in their twenties, they won't develop a reliance on pure power. They are forced to discover another way to win.

This is not, however, only a book for the newcomer. It's intended for players who need to improve or who face developing a game suited to their age. They might be right at the turning point where they are slowly discovering people they used to beat regularly are now winning.

This book is not a substitute for a good professional. It's an excellent tool for the pro, experienced in dealing with senior players, to use for skull practice during off-the-court sessions. It's also a book for you to study while taking lessons because many of the things you are shown will be presented here in different words.

Tennis is a game. It's a life-style for some, but it's a game. A sport. You do it because it's fun. Sure, it helps you keep in shape, makes you think, and calls upon your physical stamina. But if it weren't fun, you probably wouldn't be too interested in playing.

The purpose of this book is to make tennis more fun. If we manage to do this, in any way, then you've gotten something from our work.

Since we're professionals, and a part of the profession we practice is teaching, we get real satisfaction out of your added enjoyment from the greatest game in the world.

J.M. and R.S.

A NOTE ON HOW THIS BOOK WAS WRITTEN

In writing this book, Jason, Russell, and I stumbled into an interesting working arrangement.

The three of us would meet somewhere by ourselves and would agree on a subject. Then Russell and Jason would start talking to each other while I sat quietly, taking notes. The only time I would interrupt was when one of them made a point I felt needed elaboration. Then they would both explain their precise meanings and, without urging, go back into their discussion.

Thinking back, I recall the early morning when we three met in a small country town cafe, The Cottonwood Inn, near La Grange, Texas. We'd selected the place because it was about halfway between Houston and Austin, an equal drive for all of us. Russell's red Porsche was already parked outside when Jason and I drove up, about 7:30 A.M., just after a spectacular sunrise.

They talked about mental toughness while putting away huge platters of hotcakes, eggs, sausages, ham, grits, and toast. The people who ran the place were very nice and kept bringing us coffee until the conversation died about 10:00 A.M. and we ended the session.

Writing a book this way makes it a little hard to maintain a point of view. The short stories before each chapter are obviously told from a third-person position. The texts of the chapters are their ideas, comments, and experiences. Sometimes it became necessary to refer to Jason or Russell, or both together, to illustrate a point.

To simplify matters, if you'll think of the anecdotes as being told by an observer, and the instructional parts from the two champions, you won't have any trouble figuring out what's happening.

In the course of twenty years, I've worked with experts in a number of fields, and can judge when someone knows a subject. Jason and Russell know theirs. They bring to their teaching a grand enthusiasm, an appreciation for the game, and a love of playing. On top of all that, they're a couple of nice guys.

But I wouldn't want to face either one of them across a net in a tight, crucial game. They play to win. And they win by playing smarter.

C.B.

WINNING TENNIS
AFTER FORTY

1
Where, Not How

"It's not how you hit it, but where you hit it."
Jason Morton

The tall, thin, sun-browned man standing on the sidelines turned to his shorter, more thickly built companion and with a nod of his head toward the two people on the court, said in a low voice, "Her side of the net's got so many bloody balls it looks like a daisy patch." Russell Seymour spoke with clipped precision. Not even the many years he'd spent in the United States had completely robbed him of his slight English accent.

Jason Morton smiled, his grin lighting up a normally serious face. "But she's got a beautiful stroke. Looks like something out of a picture book." The sound of Texas was in every word.

The two, just returned from their unprecedented fifth National Senior Singles and Doubles Championship victories, were watching a young pro work with a woman in her mid-forties. What each of them was seeing can be classed as one of the major problems in coaching the older player.

After each shot, the attractive woman, who wore a neat orange one-piece skirt and blouse, would turn to her teacher, her face a study in concern. "How did that look?"

"Looking fine. Here comes another one."

The catapult arm of the green ball machine snapped forward, throwing a precise shot into her deep backcourt. She moved gracefully into

1

position, planted herself, and executed a classic backhand. There was a solid thunk as she caught it with her racket. Then, an instant after her exceptionally clean follow-through, there came a deader sound as the yellow ball hit the net two inches below the top and bounced languidly to the ocher clay of the court.

Unconcerned, she glanced toward her pro. "Did that look right?"

He nodded, smiling. "Great style."

Both turned to face the still-humming throwing machine. "Keep a little more weight on your back foot." The woman nodded as she settled herself for the next return. She spoke without looking. "We'll have to stop after this one and pick up the balls. There're so many on this side of the net it's getting hard to run."

"Hit this one, then we'll take a break."

Russell looked down at the stocky, athletically built Morton, shaking his head. "There ought to be a bloody break all right. But it should be somebody breaking that young man's head."

She met the next pitch easily, hitting solidly after the first bounce. The ball sailed over the net, clearing it by a good two feet. With little drop in its trajectory, it landed a foot behind the base line, out of bounds.

"Damn!" It was a sharply whispered exclamation, but it carried over to where the two men were still standing. The lady's face showed her vexation. Emotion sharpened her voice. "Just out. A foot shorter and I'd've had it." Her voice softened. "How'd I look?"

"Great. Good backhand. Real style."

Mollified, she bent over and started picking up the balls scattered thickly on her side of the net. The instructor moved toward Jason and Russell to get the chrome wire cage ball retriever. Frowning, the two men, engaged in animated conversation, turned, and walked back toward the clubhouse.

LOOKING RIGHT CAN BE WRONG

A common fault made by both students and coaches is concisely illustrated by the sentence: "Did that look right?"

Concern about how a shot looks is a mistake. The effort to emulate somebody else's classic idea of a swing or service will disrupt the natural flow inherent in each of us and can cause a measurable loss of efficiency and accuracy.

Beginners, naturally, need a sound base from which to start, so there has to be an elementary model. But as soon as a novice has developed a little control, settled on a grip, and learned the principles of good balance, he should be encouraged to find a personal style.

Tennis matches are not won by paying attention to how you hit the ball or how you look hitting the ball.

VICTORY COMES FROM SELECTING WHERE TO HIT THE BALL

Where, not how, is the single most vital concept the older player can gain. Asking how your stroke looked instead of concentrating on the exactness of positioning the return is a habit which is guaranteed to lose matches.

There is no "right" or "wrong" way to stroke the ball. If a technique is effective for you, then by definition it is your right way. You should use it without any thought about how it deviates from the standard basic teaching. Anything else is wrong.

Watching the top touring professionals play against each other can be revealing. Few of them exhibit a classic style. All, to the limits of their athletic ability, possess a fluid smoothness which clearly shows they have practiced until the motion of the stroke is automatic. They are concentrating on where to hit the next return, paying no attention at all to how they look while doing it.

If you start a list of exceptional players and their eccentricities of style, you'll end up with every big name in the game today. And yesterday, too, for that matter.

Bjorn Borg doesn't do anything classically except win consistently. Since winning is what everyone is trying to do, that may mean his style is very classic indeed.

Eddie Dibbs is another "all wrong" player. He has a backhand like a baseball batter's. All his weight is on his back foot so he gets everything into the swing. No one could possibly give him many points on style but the roundhouse power stroke comes off hard, fast, and accurate.

The enigmatic Harold Solomon is another example. His play is original. Early in his career he was told by a well-meaning pro, "You'll never be a top contender unless you learn to volley." Harold's been a seeded player in so many tournaments it's hard to count them. Yet he is still not a volley artist. He doesn't need to be, because he plays his own game.

If you want to be a winner, you have to learn to play yours too. By the time you are forty and have been playing for a number of years, you've probably developed some strong ideas about the game and how to win it. Those ideas, though, which worked well when you were twenty-five or even thirty-five, might not be so effective as you grow older.

The player who has always been able to win points by blasting the ball past every opponent suddenly hits it one day and the younger person on the other side of the net easily returns it. The ball which was once a blaster is now almost a blooper. Obviously, a change in tactics is needed to compensate for the lost power.

THE COURT GETS BIGGER

Take the players who have been able to cover their court like green on grass. If a ball landed in bounds, chances are they would be able to return it. Something happens to the size of the court after forty. Russell Seymour said it best when talking about playing Cliff Drysdale, a man eleven years his junior. "I don't know for certain what happened, but the court on my side of the net was bigger than his. It took me a lot longer to move from one part to another." He was recognizing some loss of his previous speed and his ability to set up for every shot in time to make it well.

REEVALUATE YOUR GAME

Compensating for lessening physical ability starts with a reevaluation of your game, not with a reconstruction of your form. The only time you should consider altering your basic stroke is when the stroke consistently no longer does the job. If it's not working and scoring, you've got nothing to lose in trying something else.

But first, before you start experimenting, think through your game. If you're playing with the same tactics and mental attitude you used ten years ago, you need a change.

ACCURACY GIVES YOU POINTS

Developing a new playing strategy sounds easy, but it isn't. It's simple to say accurate ball placement, but difficult to achieve it. No matter how hard you can hit, or how fast you cover the court, sooner or later your game is going to depend upon accuracy more than any other single skill. Once you can hit the ball where you want it to go time after time, you will be in a position to control your opponent's returns. And once you force your opponent into a predetermined response you can counter with a shot which has better odds of winning the point.

FIRST GET THE BALL OVER THE NET!

Accurate placement starts by getting the ball over the net. It's astounding how many otherwise excellent players will scream, bitch, and moan when their well-placed return lands a foot out of bounds, but will say nothing and not even be upset when the shot hits the net. The point is lost either way, but a net ball doesn't seem as traumatic to most people.

The ball which fails to enter the opposition's court is worse than the out-of-bounds shot. If the ball makes it over the net, even if it is clearly going to be out, there is always the possibility some dummy will return it, keeping you alive. Better still, they might try to hit it back from an awkward position due to the high path of the ball and give you a setup. Even if they let it go, there is more pressure on your opponent when the ball crosses the net than when the point is lost by its failing to do so. Keeping pressure on the other side is a vital part of playing a winning game.

Some people think clearing the net by an inch or two every shot is a mark of a skilled, class player. It's actually the sign of someone who would rather show off a mistaken idea of style than win. Flirting with the net by just clearing it has its place when your opponent is in the forecourt, but at most other times it's just a good way to lose a point or two.

A shot which makes it over has four things going for it. Gravity will carry it down somewhere, so the ball may stay in bounds, it could land with spin on it, the wind might help you, and your opponent will be tempted to keep it in play.

PUT THE BALL WHERE YOU WANT IT TO GO

There's more to accurate ball placement than getting the shot into your opponent's territory. Placement will help cause a number of unforced errors.

Most players are beaten by the mistakes they make, on their own, in response to the opposition's game. By reducing the frequency of unforced errors by only 20 percent, many would find themselves winning 40 percent more games.

Practicing shot accuracy is not a difficult accomplishment. In addition to the drills at the end of this chapter, you can improve your skill by concentrating while playing to recognize if you are reliably able to put the ball where you intended it to go.

The real difference between two players of equal athletic ability who are forty or older is the success in placing each shot into a predetermined area.

YOU *CAN* KEEP IT UP ALL DAY

One of the greatest enemies of accuracy is tension. This muscle-tightening nervous reaction ruins the fluid motion necessary to generate force without effort, which, in turn, causes the ball to go astray. A single thought, "I have to win this point," can produce sufficient reaction among some players to ensure its loss.

Another cause of tense play is success. It's almost a case of too much of a good thing.

Say you've scored three points in a row. Now, waiting for the serve, your mind begins to wander a bit. "I've made three. There's a good chance I'm going to miss this one, because I can't keep it up all day." What has happened is you have allowed yourself to fall prey to "series thinking." Sadly enough, it doesn't work the opposite way. If you've missed three in a row, you don't get the feeling the next one is yours. Unless you are very careful, your mental attitude will pull the rug out from under your skill and you won't make many more points in the game.

THE FALLACY OF SERIES THINKING

The smart player realizes points in a tennis match are like money bet on poker. The same people who begin to feel shaky having scored three or four in a row would never, in a game of five-card draw where they failed to fill an inside straight and wind up with a pair of threes, push more money into the pot just because they already had a few dollars invested in the game. They would not follow good money with bad when chances for success were at best poor.

The same holds true in tennis. But we have to make ourselves believe it. If you've taken three in a row, forget about it. The next point is a new situation, like a new hand of cards. You have to make yourself disregard what has just occurred as far as scoring and concentrate all your attention onto the ball coming into play. What you should recall are observed strengths and weaknesses of your opponent, not some vague statistical fear your time is up and you are going to lose one.

The "ball-series" syndrome doesn't stop at three. If you run your string to six or seven, the fear will still be there, nagging at the back of your mind. If you don't take control by centering your thoughts on the flight of the ball, it will control you. An unforced error is almost certain to result.

WIN BY BALL PLACEMENT AND MENTAL ATTITUDE

Winning tennis, then, for the over-forty player, is a matter of ball placement and mental attitude. The same might be said for the under-forty enthusiast, too, but the younger stroker still has the stamina, added speed, and extra power to rely on hitting through, playing base line to base line. What the senior competitor has is experience, skill, mental attitude, and accurate ball placement.

Does it work? Can the forty-plus man or woman still beat a younger competitor of equal skill? Bobby Riggs is living proof. He is capable of facing opponents half his age and winning. Some of his strokes look unorthodox, but they work for him. His ball placement is nearly miraculous.

COORDINATION CAN BE LEARNED

Riggs brings us to another point. He is a well-coordinated man. All of us aren't so lucky. Coordination is vital to anyone who wishes to play winning tennis. Even if you've played for years, two left feet or fingers that are all thumbs will stymie your progress. Coordination is the big difference between those who are considered to be athletic and nonathletic. To a large extent, depending on how hard you are willing to work and train, coordination can be learned. But people with natural ability in this area have to be taught differently from those with little inherent coordination. Well-developed players can be brought along more rapidly as they will assimilate the many variables of the traveling ball quicker.

A tennis ball in flight is a vagrant, rascally thing. A player waiting or moving to receive it must compute its speed, probable bounce height, court position, wind factors, location of opponents, and a number of other things in a few milliseconds. Then, without conscious thought, respond automatically and place the shot. There is only a limited time to assess the data, interpret it, and decide on the play.

People with normal or even slightly subnormal coordination can be brought up to high levels of ability through concentrated practice and work with an understanding professional. While they may never become national senior champions, they will be able to win matches from far more coordinated people who don't work as hard at the game.

IT'S BETTER TO BE THE WINNER

Throughout this chapter winning has come up time and time again. And for good reason. Tennis is a contest. There is, at the end, as in every contest, a winner and a loser. Experience has taught us all it is better to be the winner.

There are other rewards inherent in the game. The feel of a good fluid stroke, the placement of a ball which causes a chain of events predetermined by your mind, the scoring of a hard point—these are only a few of the positives.

All of us, each in our own minds, recognize there is something else: the triumph of winning. Not beating the other player, but winning. Coming out on top because you exercised your best abilities, and on that day, at that time, in that place, they were sufficient to carry you through.

Losing isn't the same as winning. Even if you've played your best and sincerely enjoyed the contest, coming in second feels like being beaten. This isn't necessarily negative. In many cases the bitter taste is just the spur lots of people need to force an improvement in their games.

Winning is more fun than losing. Since we play for fun, we should play to win at least our share of the matches, which means playing to win every point in every game.

If you do this, and play point by point, you'll end up with the right attitude to be a winner. If you play smart, focusing on where you put the ball as opposed to how you look hitting it, work out a strategy which allows you to play within your ability, and concentrate on eliminating unforced errors, you'll win more games than you lose, and have more fun playing.

SUGGESTED DRILLS AND PRACTICE

The Phantom Net

One of the best ways to get the ball over the net is to imagine another net along your opponent's service line. Instead of trying to skim the real barrier when your opposition is in the backcourt, force yourself to keep your shot high enough to make it over the imaginary second net.

Someone hitting to you or the use of a ball machine will allow you to try this a number of times. *A successful practice period will not find a single ball on your side of the real net.* It's a hard goal, but your unforced error problem will be greatly reduced by attaining it.

A Real Target

One good way to develop ball placement is to put an object into the far court and try to actually hit it while serving. The same thing can be done during a return of balls. Some people use the intersection of two lines on the court or an imaginary spot, but a real object, small enough to be knocked over or tossed up into the air when the ball strikes it, has an interesting psychological effect. It sounds a little odd, and people might laugh at you, but try it. If you like it, do it again. It may psych a few players out, and you can pick up a couple of easy games.

The Twenty-Ball Test

Drills designed to get you to move in each direction while still maintaining accurate returns are also a must.

Get someone to hit twenty balls to you in rapid-fire sequence. The pace should be such as to force you to keep moving at all times. Each ball should be aimed at a different part of your court so you are constantly in motion, back and forth. When you hit the return, aim it. Imagine an opponent in motion as well and place the ball in the most strategic position. Twenty balls, if this is done right, is an exhausting exercise. You can keep two scores to monitor your progress: (1) how many fail to cross the net and (2) how many times your shot lands where you intended.

The Thinker in Action

Practice of your on-court position can be added to the last drill by having your partner hit the balls in a set sequence. A pattern might run: backcourt; forecourt; left side, deep; right side, shallow; down the line; lob. Aware of the pattern, you can evaluate your court position after each stroke to determine where you are against where you need to be. Learning the most efficient and economic way to get from one point to another inside the white lines may not seem to be a problem, but for some people, it requires practice. Court position is a key to an effective return.

Ken Rosewall is the epitome of the player who has mastered this. In addition to being quick, he is agile. His footwork is tremendous, and his anticipation of an opponent's next move is almost uncanny. Much of his ability is directly due to his thinking while he plays and to consciously selecting the most advantageous position on the court in light of the previous shots his opponent has made in response to his returns.

The position you select in the instant after you hit the ball back can affect your winning or losing. Practice can improve your ability in this vital area.

Several of the following game situation drills can give you the practice needed to master return shots from various positions on the court. In these workouts the goal of each player should be to keep the ball in play. Accuracy is the primary consideration. Go through these routines at a comfortable pace. Don't rush. Focus your attention on the ball, the shot you are making, and where it is supposed to go.

Four-Player Rotation

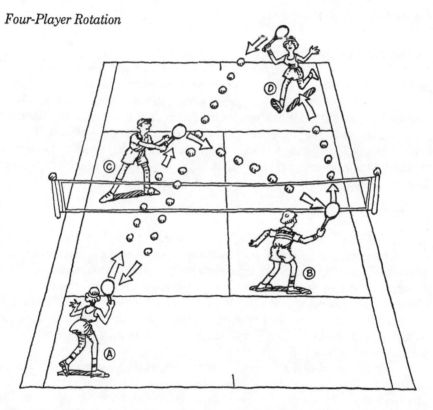

Using four players (A, B, C, and D), A and B are on the same side of the court at the base line while C and D are on the other side of the court at the net. A, back, is opposite C, net. A hits to C, who takes it as a volley, returning it to B, who knocks it to D, who volleys it to A, allowing the sequence to start again. The players at the net volley, the players at the base line return.

After your group has learned to keep the ball in play for long periods, you can switch by having one of the four call out, "Change." The two at the net retreat to their base line and the two who were back come forward to volley.

Two-Player Rotation

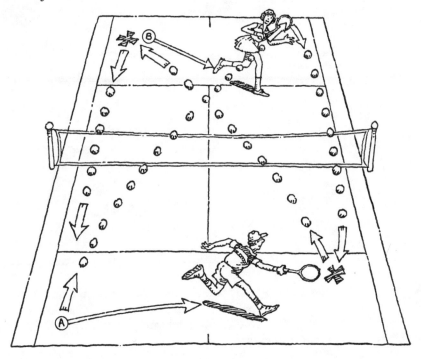

A and B are both in their backcourts, opposite one another. A starts the practice by hitting a well-placed ball to B's opposite court, causing B to run parallel to the net to make the shot. B should return the ball straight down the line, and A, in anticipation, should practice moving to where the ball will land. A then returns the ball to B's original position, which moves B over again. B should also start to move into position, practicing easy court movement and anticipation. B's return will be to A's original position, causing A to start back as soon as the shot is made.

Remember, the object is accuracy and keeping the ball in play.

Hitting across the court will show you why pros say the cross-court player is in command. The distance is longer, the angles better, and the center of the net is lower.

Three-Player Rotation

A and B are midcourt on the same side. C is midcourt over the net. A hits to C's backhand. C returns the ball to B, who hits to C's forehand. Make ten complete cycles: A to C to B to C to A, then switch off positions. No running in this one if everyone is accurate.

Poacher's Paradise

A and B are on one side, C and D on the other. A is at the base line in a service position, B is in the other court, at the net. C is back to receive A's serve, D is midcourt on C's side. A serves softly to C, who hits between A and B. B moves over, poaching, to pick off the shot and hit it to D's feet, to allow D to block the shot or to intercept in turn. D sends the ball back to A to be served again. Three times and everyone rotates positions.

Senior players should take special notice of this drill. The older players get, the less inclined they seem to be to poach. Work at it. Keep both the ability and the inclination. It will win you games.

Poacher's Paradise

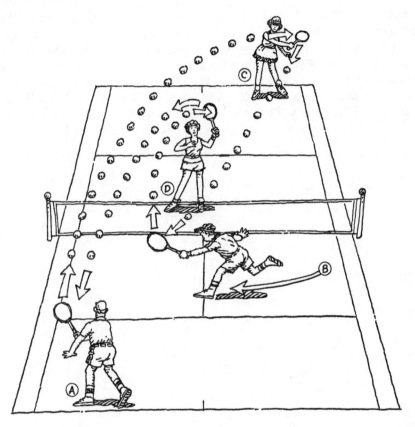

Strategy

Superior strategy will also help you win. Remember one thing when you start to develop a game plan. The most complex, Machiavellian schemes won't work as well as simple, properly executed programs which have as their base an observed fact. A player with a weak serve, for instance, is probably going to have a poor overhead return. Or if you're playing outdoors and the sun is in your opponent's face, lob a lot. Don't make a low return. Keep lobbing. Sooner or later there will be an unforced error which will give you a point.

Keep your strategy simple. If it's based on reality, it'll win.

2
Learning After Forty Is Easier

"I have a little dream of being the first forty-nine-year-old player to win Wimbledon. I know it's only a dream, but there are some days it seems just possible."
Russell Seymour

Hotel and motel lobbies have a sameness early in the morning. The late-night skeleton crew is at the end of its duty, and the clerks, not harassed by the demands of arriving or departing guests, move methodically, performing mysterious tasks with paper slips in their narrow, behind-the-counter world.

Jason Morton strode across the lobby of the Marriott toward the restaurant, alone with his postdawn thoughts. As a younger player, he'd won his share of matches but had never been nationally ranked. Now, after the Charlottesville Tournament, he was the Senior Men's National Singles and Doubles Clay Court Champion. He'd won it going away just the month before. He entered the coffee shop wearing his usual grin. It was a good day and he was looking forward to his first match in the National Senior Men's Grass Tournament. If I just don't get too many crazy bounces, he thought, keep my mind on the game . . . His chain of reverie was broken by the hostess who approached with brightly colored menus and a radiant smile.

"One, sir? Right this way." She had already started back to the tables she guarded as she spoke. Morton trailed behind as the two of them moved through the crowded establishment.

"Jason. Come join us."

The voice startled him, so he stopped. The hostess, thinking he

15

was still following, moved away, her eye on a small double near the back wall.

Seated, drinking coffee, were David Markin, president of Checker Manufacturing Company, and Gunther Balz, his regular doubles partner. David, an avid senior tournament competitor, was the national director of the Junior Davis Cup and active in a variety of tennis organizations. Gunther, winner of several National Unlimited Air Races, was also rated as a fine player.

Nodding to the two men, Jason took a seat, staring back over his shoulder trying to find the now-vanished hostess. A waitress arrived. Without asking, she placed a glass of water, a white paper napkin wrapped around tableware, and a brimming cup of black, hot coffee onto the plastic place mat in front of him. "I'll be back to get your order in a minute." The way she said it, the words seemed like a single expression.

Jason turned to Markin. "Sorry you had to leave the tournament early. You missed a good show."

"I'm sorry, too, Jason. Family emergency. Who finally won the singles?"

Morton smiled. "I did."

There was a long pause. Markin seemed puzzled. "Oh, come on, Jason. You had me for a minute there. Who really took it?"

"I won it."

The silence was a little longer. Markin turned to Balz. "You think he's kidding?"

Balz shook his head. "Doesn't sound like it to me."

"You really win it, Jason?"

Smiling even more, Morton nodded. "I really won it."

Markin broke into a huge grin. Laughing, he banged the table with excitement. "I'll tell you one thing, Jason. I couldn't be happier. Your winning gives hope to every hacker in the world!"

IT'S TIME TO PLAY HARDER AND SMARTER

Psychiatrists and psychologists tell us the fortieth birthday is a traumatic point in life for most people. Somehow forty is a natural dividing line. You wake up one morning and, unless you are one of the chosen few, there is more of your life behind you than there is waiting ahead. You inventory what you've achieved, compare it to the goals and aspirations you formed as a youth, and, if you're like many of us, you come up short. You realize time is running out so if you're ever going to attain even a semblance of your original dreams, you'd better get after it.

People over forty tend to rededicate their lives as they focus more carefully on desired achievements. They work, in most cases, harder and smarter. They get more done with less wasted motion or thrashing about. For most things, they still have excellent command of their physical faculties.

Lots of good tennis players come into their own after their fortieth birthdays. Since they work hard, they tend to play hard, too. The same rededication carries over into their game. They show marked improvement in concentration and develop a winning mental attitude.

On the physical side, however, tennis is more demanding than most of life's other tasks. The older player runs into a barrier of time. Body flexibility and reflex reaction time are lost. The ace server can't bend his back or reach quite as high as he could at twenty. Or even thirty. The woman who could cover the court by springing from one side to the other now finds some of the spring sprung. You can't bend down as low as you used to, so more and more shots fall just out of your most exerted reach. Heated rallies don't seem to last as long, either.

If you've had any of these experiences, you're not alone. But don't despair too much for lost youth. Over-forty players, beginners or long-term enthusiasts, can, in most cases, play as good a tennis game now as they did when they were in their thirties, if they play with their brains as opposed to their brawn.

YOU HAVE SOME ADVANTAGES

Older players have several advantages when they try to start learning the game or begin retraining their skills. First, they are not as likely as the young enthusiast to be trying to impress someone. We all start out as children with a look-at-me attitude, and it takes some years to get it all under control. The over-forty player should have mastered this urge, so any desire to show off ought to be long dead or very, very dormant.

Second, as a forty-plus-year-old player you have a good understanding of your personal limitations, in both a physical and a mental sense. Think back to when you were twenty. Or thirty. Compare your present feelings about the maximum you are willing to exert yourself today with then. Some people get quite a shock realizing how little control they exercised over their physical selves for a long period of their lives. Today, you know you're not ever going to beat a touring pro Love-Love. But back then, on a day when you were hot, and since everyone knew you as one of the top players in the club, maybe, just maybe . . . You get the idea. Today you understand your physical limitations better. If you don't, you must learn to.

The understanding of your mental limits is also vital. Generally, people over forty have a clear picture of who they are, which goes with a strong sense of how they relate to society. This allows posturing and striving to stop and gives the individual more time to concentrate on important things. One generality drawn from decades of active coaching is that players who win with great frequency share a common sense of directness and honesty. They seldom kid themselves, because they can't and win. They are forced to face facts, accept them, then plan accordingly to allow their game to overcome an opponent's greater strength or agility. Winning players know who they are. They have a strong sense of personal identity without an overwhelmingly egocentric orientation. By the time we are forty or older, most of us have a deep-down realistic conception of ourselves.

Older players have another edge going for them. They are able to concentrate for a longer period of time, and it takes more of an outside distraction to pull their minds away from what they are doing. Concentration, as will be discussed later, is a part of an overall attitude we call *Mental Toughness*. It alone can make the difference between a winning and losing player.

Many matches between senior players are won by the less skillful contestant, even on days when the opponent is hot, because only one person on the court truly cared about winning. It's all right to be a graceful loser, but it's nicer, at least for most of us, to be gracious winners.

Bill Tym, a good athlete, comes to mind when winning attitude is discussed. Bill played a world-class Yugoslav one time and could have beaten him. But the young Slav wanted to win so badly he overcame the difference in playing skills through concentration.

Everyone has the potential ability to fix his mind on a subject and to stay with it. The older player is, after training, simply able to do it longer, break it less frequently, and return to it more quickly.

A final superiority held by forty-plus individuals is, or should be, an ability to establish reasonable, attainable goals. Senior players are able to decide how much time they wish to devote to the game, estimate the speed of their progress, then define levels of achievement which fall within their physical, mental, and temporal reach.

If every player set realistic standards, then worked toward them, the quality of tennis would improve overnight. And people would be getting more enjoyment from the game.

A THOUGHTFUL PRO CAN RETRAIN YOUR THINKING

Over-forty individuals who want to play winning tennis need to find a pro who understands their problem. Proper lessons for both new and seasoned players need to center more on philosophy, less on technique. They need to be drilled in the mental side of the game to teach their minds to do half the work by planning strategy which imposes their strengths on the opposition's weaknesses.

The over-forty player can be a better balanced competitor who plays all aspects of the game equally, relying less on sheer strength.

Thoughtful coaching can retrain thinking. Consider the importance of lobs and drop shots, for example. In the younger player's book, these are dangerous. Agile, youthful hitters can, if they try, run most of them down to deliver killing returns. Among the older players, where things have slowed up a bit, more and more of those deep lobs go untouched. It's just too physically taxing to move into position. A drop shot, of marginal use when you were thirty, becomes a part of your repertory at forty-five as a scoring tool.

PLAY THE BALL, DON'T JUST WATCH IT

Senior players run into another barrier coaching can help. As their physical game declines, many tend to become "reflex hitters," who stand in one place, make a shot, then, without trying to anticipate where the return might come, stop to watch the game. It's almost as if they take a time-out. Once their opponent hits the ball, they react reflexively, scrambling to put a racket on it. The late start causes them to miss returns they would have made easily in their younger days. They begin to feel they've lost their ability to move, when they are still capable of getting around.

All reflex players are experiencing a physical manifestation of a mental problem stemming from laziness. The head is not being used as much as the feet. Careful coaching can pull an individual out of the doldrums and restore confidence.

TACTICS BECOME VITAL SIGNS

While tactics are necessary in every game, regardless of the ages of the players, they are of vital importance to the over-forties. They take on a new meaning because as physical limitations cut into the number of possible shots and returns which can be made in a match, the other player's responses become more predictable. It's easier to guess what will come next and start moving into a position to cover the return before it's made. You've got to stay alert. Work on anticipation can put you well ahead in any close contest.

POSITION IS EVERYTHING IN TENNIS AND LIFE

Court position is a more important factor in over-forties games. With two senior players, action will usually occur farther back from the net than it would with younger people. A couple of good tips on positioning yourself are included in the various drill sections of this book.

Another consideration with which the forty-plus player must contend is the decision when to go hard and when to back off. Every game has crucial points where an all out effort for only a brief period will produce positive results. Rushing the net after you return a serve on an ad point, for instance, alert and ready, applies pressure to your opponent. This pressure, all by itself, can often be enough to cause a mistake at a crucial time. A sudden change in your pacing of the game can be highly effective against some people who can be led by your actions. It's worth a try in the early stages of the contest. If it works, you've got a trick when you need it.

ENDURANCE SCORES MORE THAN CHANCES

One of the common faults of the over-forties man or woman relearning their game is to overplay the ball. In the heat of a rally they get excited or become anxious for the rapid-fire chain of events to end. This causes a desire to take a chance on making a shot which might, just might, have a marginal opportunity to put the ball away. Players of all ages do it frequently. Seniors, however, should be able to remain calm enough to avoid the pressure, close down that part of their minds calling for an end to the tension, and keep the ball in play.

Each time you hit it across the net, only two things can happen. You'll make the point or get it banged back at you. Concentrating on keeping the action moving will prevent you from taking the poor-risk shot, so sooner or later, if you stay with it, you'll get an opportunity to score.

PERFECT THE STROKES THAT MADE POINTS FOR YEARS

Down in Texas there is a saying which originated in the days of the country square dances. A swain would bring his wife or date for the evening to the affair and if she were at all attractive, several of the available men would make a run at her to see if they could sign her up for dances. A ladylike response was, "Thank you, but I'll dance with who brung me." It meant she was loyal to her escort. Dancing with who brung you is a good rule for over-forty players, too.

Everyone who has played for any time has certain shots that have been reliable standbys in their games. These may need minor modification, but unless they are based on pure power, chances are they'll still be effective. You might find it necessary, especially to increase accuracy, to cut back on the force of your smash. Instead of striking with all your energy, you might reduce the effort to 70 or 80 percent, which helps timing and compensates for slowing reactions.

You previously may have been able to induce spin by your stroke. Now you may find it more accurate to forgo this by flattening the angle at which the racket contacts the ball. You'll still be punching out an effective shot, but more important, you'll be making it land where you want. It's still a good arrow in your quiver. Dance with who brung you. Don't give up the strokes that made points for years. Modify them a little, as necessary with the passage of time. If you don't change at all, sooner or later you're going to be in for big trouble.

ILLOGICAL PLAYING COSTS POINTS

The game of tennis is logical. The player who uses logic will win. It's illogical to try to make shots beyond your present physical limitations. Do it and a less talented opponent will beat you. The same is true for tactics. If you take chances on the court, you'll be a sitting duck. Play conservatively and you'll win more than your share.

LOSE FEWER POINTS AND WIN MORE GAMES

One final point about learning, or relearning, the game after forty. The senior player is more amenable to accepting facts. Experience has trained the mind to evaluate a situation and make an informed decision. Basic truths are more easily grasped.

The one basic truth: *More points are lost than won.*

The number of times unforced errors lose a point will be far more than the spectacular put-away shots which cannot be returned, no matter what. The player who loses the fewest number of points from simple mistakes, lack of concentration, or negligence will usually come out the winner.

THREE PRINCIPLES THAT WILL PAY OFF

Principle Number One, for Singles

First is the idea of a home base. Pick a spot four to five feet behind the base line right in the dead middle of the court. Get to know it because you should be spending a lot of time here. Stand in one place. Look around. Like the neighborhood? You'd better. It's where the winners live. This position is your home base from now on. It's the place to which you naturally gravitate when there is any doubt about where your opponent is going to hit the ball.

The reason is easy to see if you try something. Stand ready. Imagine a ball landing at the extreme edge of the court to your right. You can get to it by moving halfway across, because you're already half there. Same with a ball to your left. Picture a high one coming in. You'll be in the best position to judge its impact point and therefore decide to take it or pass. One which drops just over the net? You'll have a full bounce as you move forward.

Now, move off to one side about three feet. Look how much open court you've left undefended. If an opponent shows a consistent tendency to hit to one side, you can move over, but watch out. It's an old sucker play to lure a center-placed player off base.

Principle Number Two, for Doubles

Now the home base becomes the center of the court you're supposed to be defending. That's easy. The hard part is moving in unison with your partner.

Doubles players should be like a pair of riders on a tandem bicycle. When one pushes down on a pedal, the other is doing the same thing. In tennis, wherever you find one of a pair, the other should be in a corresponding position. You go to the net, your partner follows. Your teammate falls back, you fall back, too. Playing out of sync consistently gives the other side the opportunity of applying pressure to one of you. And two on one is hardly fair in love or war.

Here's an example: You start to the net but your partner stays at the back boundary. The return is to you, toward the middle. You move over to take it, getting a clean hit. Their return is at your far boundary causing you to run to get into position, because, playing up close, this ball is yours, too. The next shot they send brings you even farther across the center line, making you hustle to get there. Their hits are soft, keeping the ball just over the net, clearly in your territory. Your partner will be afraid to move in because by this time you'll be running back and forth at a terrific rate as your opposition increases the tempo. In this situation you're sure to lose a point eventually because you're having to hit on the run, while each of your opponents is able to play a half court, moving smoothly onto the ball no matter where you place it. The only way out is for your companion to jump in, go parallel with you in reference to the net, and fill in the empty spot.

Principle Number Three, for Singles or Doubles

A ball your opponent plays from the backcourt at the far left or right boundary line will come back to one of three general areas. It all depends on how desperate your opposition is. Where he plays it will give you a clue to his probable mental outlook on his chances of winning.

Your opponent takes the ball a couple of feet in from the service line, actually having to step a few feet out of bounds to your far left-hand side of the court.

The safest stroke is a return across the center into the diagonally opposite court. It's the best angle, the flight path of the ball will be impeded only by the lowest part of the net, and there is room to smack it.

A much lower percentage shot, and therefore a desperation try, would be to hit down the line, toward the corner pocket. The ball crosses a higher portion of the net, travels a long distance over out-of-bounds territory, and must land in a small-scoring area made up of the intersection of the court's out-of-bounds lines. Not impossible, but a much harder shot to make. It's a good one, though, if you allow yourself to be caught flat-footed awaiting the expected cross-court reply.

The third possibility, and one with lower odds for success, is more aggressive. The opponent hits across the center of the net, as if going for your far corner, but makes the ball go over at a greater angle causing it to land inside the boundary line two or three feet back. A drop shot with tremendous control is needed to accomplish this and there is a risk of its going out. If it succeeds, however, you'll be faced with having to move off court and forward to respond.

If your opponent or opponents are steady players who usually take the odds-on shot, the second or third of these responses might indicate they are hungry for a point.

One final thought for doubles: The principle of moving together applies to sideways as well as forward and back. If you get stuck with your partner way off on the left side of the court and you're over to the extreme right, the middle is open. Count yourselves lucky if you cover all the returns until you establish yourselves in the center again.

Remember, wherever the one goes, you both go. Play like there is a rope around each of your waists, tying you to your teammate.

3
It's Important to Be Competitive

"Competition is the backbone of every successful tennis club. Without competitive events which interest the members, every club would wither and die. Tennis is competition and the players who compete hardest enjoy the game most." Jason Morton and Russell Seymour

It was a magnificent New York Saturday morning. The green countryside was bathed in golden sunlight producing a temperature a little less than seventy degrees. There was only the slightest breeze. Even the birds, high in the tall trees lining the sides of the clay courts, sang brighter.

Two players faced each other over the net. Both solemnly shook hands, then, carrying two huge baskets of balls, they moved into their backcourt areas.

Everything about them was perfect. The cut and fit of their expensive tennis clothes went with the pristine whiteness of their almost new shoes. Each had a racket costing at least two hundred dollars, selected with care from the pro shop.

The club and its grounds matched the two players' fineness. Manicured lawns were broken only by meticulously placed red brick walks. Waiters in gray jackets could be seen here and there, carrying drinks on small silver trays. In the parking lot, Mercedes-Benz after Mercedes-Benz was stabled next to Cadillacs, the more exotic Ferraris, and the most haughty Rolls. Porsches were as common as Volkswagens in rush-hour freeway traffic.

The two players, reaching their respective positions, placed their shiny chrome wire baskets down onto the yellow red of the clay. White lines, renewed just for this game, stood sharply in contrast to the rest of the court. Smiling, one of the two reached down and selected a yellow ball from the multicolored assortment at his disposal. Without warning, he bounced it on the ground and on the rebound, struck a roundhouse blow knocking it high in the air. The opposing player, a good-looking woman with long blond hair, didn't seem to notice. She ignored the shot, purposefully selecting a ball of her own. Choosing a green one, she threw it into the air. Smashing down, she watched the green streak fly over the net, touching behind the base line.

No one called "out" or seemed concerned.

Each player was armed with a hundred balls. They proceeded, one at a time, to knock them over the net at random. No attention was paid to where they went or even to each other, except for one occasion when, seeing a ball the woman had hit was going to bounce up near him, the man, taking a half step, slammed it back onto her side. She made no attempt to respond, and her eyes didn't follow the flight path of the return. She was intent on selecting her next ball and hitting it over.

Their methodical play kept up for a full five minutes before another exchange occurred. He hit a ball which came close to her and, seemingly on impulse, she picked it off in midair. He returned the volley. Since the ball was again presented to her and she didn't have to move, she hit it back over. It was a good shot, but a little high. The man could have smashed it down for an easy point. Instead, he seemed to lose interest, returning, with a fixed look of determination on his face, to hitting over the balls he chose from his chrome basket.

After thirty minutes he was done. He waited while the girl finished hers. Then he spoke in a gentle voice. "Good game." He sounded enthusiastic. "You want to play another?"

She shook her head. "No, not today." She paused. "It really was great fun though."

"Had a good time, eh?" He was smiling.

"You bet. Don't know when I've played anyone with your style."

He lowered his head modestly. "Same goes for me, too. Like some lunch?"

He had crossed the net and was on her side, picking up her silver wire cage in one hand, helping her adjust her white and blue cable knit sweater with the other. They started toward the gate leading out of the court area. Two groundsmen had appeared and were rapidly scooping up the gaily colored tennis balls.

Arm and arm the couple walked slowly toward the neat clubhouse, still talking about the fun they'd had during the just-completed game.

COMPETITION IS THE HEART OF TENNIS

The Alice-in-Wonderland type tennis game just described never quite happened. But almost the same scene is played day after day, year after year, in widely different areas of the country, with only one difference. There is a missing element in the story game. Both players had a good time. Both succeeded in hitting a ball and both played to their levels of skill. But there was no competition. The two individuals were each out on the court, unaware of the other as far as the tennis went, doing their own thing, with no threat of consequences, penalty for bad shots, or other created problems. In short, without competition, they were involved in a pointless endeavor which can't even be called a game.

A game, by definition, needs competition.

Tennis is a game which allows for many levels of competition and a wide variety of competitive attitudes. It's also a game that has no room for anyone who does not wish to compete.

The tennis game is a "match" between two people. For forty minutes or so the two are locked into a contest from which only one will emerge the winner. To keep things interesting there are numerous little victories as each point is fought. Even in doubles it's you against someone else every time your skill is tested by having the ball fall into your court.

Competition is the heart of tennis appeal. If you took away all the strokes, rackets, fancy designer clothes, shoes, hot balls, memberships to classy clubs, and everything else which today goes with the glamour and excitement of the game, you would still have an exciting premise: two people meeting one on one in an athletic contest where the individual with the better skills, the right frame of mind, and a little luck will prevail.

COMPETITION ISN'T NEW

If you go back in history, contests with sticks and balls are a vital part of the folk heritage of every civilized country. After throwing something back and forth in a game of catch, the next natural evolution seems to be for one of the participants to get a stick and try to hit the object in the air. Tennis is an outgrowth of this basic act. The addition of boundaries adds to the difficulty and allows the limited playing area to bring specific focus on the performance of the contestants.

ACCEPTING THE COMPETITIVE SIDE OF TENNIS WILL HELP YOU WIN

When you step onto the court with a racket in your hand, you are entering a competitive event. Even if you say you are "only going to hit some back and forth," there is a competitive weight on you. No matter how you try to avoid the feeling, at some time you'll try to return your opponent's shots to score or stop a response. You are invariably happier after a series of rallies if you win the point than if your opposition takes it.

Competition is the backbone of tennis and can be used to lead a player into improving his game through goal setting and success.

In every group of players you can, after a few matches, begin to define your tennis ability relative to the rest. You will recognize there are some far better than you, some only slightly better, more at about your same level, and many who are worse. This definition is made on the basis of who conquers whom on the courts. Your ranking or placement into a position on a ladder ranging from poor to excellent is not static. If you don't improve, you will, one step at a time as players who work harder move past you, fall down the rungs. Or, if you use the impetus of competition to spur on your game, you can rise, one notch by one notch, toward the top.

Not everyone can be the "best player" because not everyone is naturally equipped with the same athletic prowess. If you dance with two left feet, were always the last one chosen for sandlot pickup softball games when you were a kid, drive a car with your mind somewhere else, and have never won even a charity drawing last prize at the church social, you probably are not possessed of the mental and physical makeup to be a champion tennis player. Don't worry about it. Damned few people are. A lack of topflight talent doesn't leave you in a hopeless position in tennis because no matter how much natural ability, or how little, you bring to the game, there is a level of play in which the competition will be right for your best efforts.

The various ranking systems which have evolved, establishing A, B, and C players, ensure you of finding competitors to tax you and whom you, in turn, will tax.

HOW TO USE COMPETITION TO IMPROVE YOUR GAME

If the competitive factor were removed from tennis, there would be no incentive at all for you to improve. And no game for you to play anyway.

Use the competitive nature of the sport to your advantage. Competition will allow you to set and meet goals which will immeasurably increase your enjoyment of, and enthusiasm for, tennis.

If you'll take a moment to list three people in your playing circle, you will have a start on using the competition in tennis to improve your game.

First, name someone you beat on a consistent basis. Not a pushover, but a player against whom, in, say, ten matches, you'd feel confident of winning at least six, or better yet, seven.

This positions you. Anyone that person can beat, you can beat, too.

Now think of a player you feel is your even-Steven equal. Out of ten matches, you'd take five and your opponent would take the other five, all things, luck included, being normal.

Finally, name an opponent who can and would take you six-four or seven-three out of ten matches. Anyone who can beat this player can beat you.

Now let's look at the bracket you've made. If you work hard on your game, and it takes mental as well as physical practice, you'll be able to measure your progress over a period of time.

The player you consider just slightly less able than you will become more so. Instead of winning four or five games out of ten, he should, slowly, but inexorably, only be able to take one or two.

The players you consider your equals should fall back until they assume the position of the weakest opponents on your list.

Those you considered a little better than yourself will become more and more your equal.

As your ability changes and is proven through winning games, move the names on your mental list and discard the bottom one. Then pick a new "better than I am by a little" and you've established your own championship ladder. You will have set attainable goals and a measurement of your capabilities outside the opinions of the professionals or your fellow players.

This system has limits. Take the case of the man who wanted to lift a cow. He started training by picking up a newborn calf every day, on the theory of gaining strength over a long period. There came a day when, no matter how many times he had picked up the one-day-older calf, he lacked the muscle to make the lift. In other words, the man increased his strength by picking up the calf each day as it grew heavier, but he was not able to alter his maximum ability to lift weight. You have an ultimate capacity to play tennis. You will never progress past it, no matter how hard you train or exert yourself.

PLAY TO YOUR FULL POTENTIAL

But your all-out capability isn't a worry. Most players never come within 50 percent of their full potential, except for occasional matches, games, sets, or even shots. Top stars play at the pinnacle of their form. Their natural maximum is higher than yours or any recreational player's will ever be. Consistent winners, who have used competition as a training aid, play in the upper half of their ability range and find no problem taking games from bunches of enthusiasts who think they are close to their capacity but aren't even halfway there.

This concept is an important one, so let's look at it another way. If you drop a brick off the top of a ten-story building and another brick out the window of an airplane flying at ten thousand feet, both bricks will hit the ground going the same speed. The falling brick has what is called a "terminal velocity." That's the maximum speed it can reach under the force exerted by gravity, due to the resistance of the air through which it falls. No matter how much harder you try, even if you throw the brick downward instead of just drop it, and you do this at a hundred thousand feet, it just can't go any faster.

There is a terminal velocity in tennis. It's the physical and mental limits of your being able to play the game imposed on you by your personal physical and mental capabilities. Every other player has a limit or terminal velocity, too.

A strikingly poor athlete, performing at close to 100 percent of his or her maximum ability, will be able to beat moderate to good athletes giving out only 30 to 50 percent of their total ability.

Using competition to establish a base for your performance and then measuring your rate of improvement by watching your progress in winning against players of lesser, equal, and superior known ability will allow you to judge your improvement and, at the same time, measure your success in playing to your maximum against your ultimate potential.

TOPPING OUT

If you go through a period when, no matter how hard you practice, you don't seem to be able to beat the one you've singled out as your goal, and the player you've selected as your equal, who before on your list was your superior, just seems to stay equal with you, you may feel you've topped out.

Don't decide too quickly. Check with your pro. Play a few sets so you can be observed by someone who has seen the top effort of many individuals. Then ask for an opinion. You may well have hit a plateau in training. These exist and are pitfalls for the unwary. A player makes the decision to improve his or her game and begins to bear down and practice. He makes almost immediately measurable progress. Week by week, month by month, his skills improve. Suddenly, they seem to level off. They may go for two or three months without a sign of progress. Then they improve a little only to level off again.

It happens all the time and it's natural. At first, your dedication and enthusiasm get you started. You mend big faults, thus showing grand progress. Once this is achieved, there are fewer areas needing work. What you are doing wrong at this stage is much harder to correct. Add this to the certainty that each alteration will only give you a minimum amount of overall game improvement, and you can easily see why the plateau effect happens.

The trick is to recognize you have only hit the slower half of your program and to be patient. Many people are fooled into thinking they have reached close to their ultimate ability, so they back off, using only enough effort to hold themselves at this stage of development.

It's a mistake, but one you may have trouble spotting yourself, without the yardstick of competition to give you an adequate measure of your still-growing ability.

THE IMPORTANCE OF A GOOD TENNIS ENVIRONMENT

Association with players who are competitive at their own levels is good for the over-forty hitter. Somehow, the added enthusiasm keeps senior players more active. The same is true for involvement in a club or program which uses competition as its main motivating force.

A good tennis environment is one where a number of competitions for various levels of skill are scheduled on a regular basis. A Valentines mixed doubles, for instance, held as an annual event, will draw larger crowds each year. It becomes an institution for many people who find satisfaction in comparing their performances with their previous recorded best.

HARNESSED COMPETITION

Harnessed competition is a force for the senior player. It can lend a new meaning to the game, provide new reasons for trying to improve, add dimensions to play, and give more enjoyment and satisfaction.

Over-forties will find competition can keep them more deeply involved in the contest, and it might become the impetus for revamping their physical conditioning efforts as they strive to achieve more success.

The older player is able to approach competition and resulting game stress with a level head. Age, in evaluating competitive limits, can be a positive advantage. Competition can make up for many difficulties and problems brought on by the years past thirty-five.

Without competition and a feeling of competitive rivalry between players, tennis wouldn't be a game. It might still be a social pastime, but it would have none of the charm, glamour, or excitement.

And it wouldn't, in all probability, have you for a player.

4
Learning How
to Win

"There are lots of good players who don't win."   Russell Seymour

When the voice came on the other end of the line, I was a little surprised. I'd expected the slight English accent which came from living and playing in South Africa and Australia, but there was an intensity and tension I hadn't anticipated. My flat Texas twang isn't too pronounced, softened as it is by my Florida drawl, but it stood out against the clipped precision of his pronunciation.

"Russell? Russell Seymour?"

"Right."

"Jason Morton. I'm the pro up at the University Club."

"I've heard of you."

"And me, you." There was a pause. He didn't seem to like to waste words in idle conversation. In response, I decided to get right down to why I was calling. "They're playing the Texas Sectionals for the Seniors over in San Antonio next month."

The lack of an answer from the other end made me feel like I'd just told him something he already knew and he was still waiting for me to get to the point. In the next couple of weeks, I'd learn he wasn't at all unfriendly. His almost brusque manner stemmed from his constant practice of concentrating very hard on what he was doing at the moment. But at the time, it made me feel a little like my son Stephen must have felt when as a teen-ager he called the class beauty queen for a date.

"They're playing the Texas Sectionals over in San Antonio, like I said, and I wanted to know if you'd team with me in doubles?"

There was a momentary pause before he replied.

"Let me see if I can arrange to get off."

It was my turn to wait and he responded quickly.

"I'll let you know."

"Thanks."

He hung up suddenly and I sat there with a buzzing telephone receiver in my hand.

We'd agreed to meet at two on the afternoon before the tournament, and Russell was as punctual as his diction was precise. I looked him over as he approached. The tan I'd expected. I had one and so does every other player who has lived in a hot climate. At about six feet, he wasn't inordinately tall, but he gave the impression of being so. His long, whipcord muscles moved under his brown skin, and his sharp greenish-brown eyes were constantly in motion. He slipped easily into the chair opposite me, sat forward, smiled, and folded his hands on top of the table.

"Jason?"

"Russell?"

"We're going to knock hell out of them."

The way he said it, I knew he meant it. But I didn't know how much.

I was disappointed when he entered the singles as well as the doubles competition. First, because I didn't want to have to play against him, and second, because I wanted us both to be ready and rested for what I consider-ed the important part of the program.

Curious to see his style, I gravitated to the court as Russell paired off with Dr. Bill Owen. Bill is a good player, has some nice shots, and isn't anybody's idea of a pushover.

The whole thing lasted about twenty minutes. Russell drubbed him Love-Love. Bill Owen barely managed to score a point in the match.

I walked away, shaking my head. Russell was good. Maybe great. But for the life of me, I couldn't see why, with the affair in hand, he couldn't have let Bill Owen have a game or two, just to make him feel better.

Later the same afternoon, after I'd won a not-too-exciting match, I spotted a seeded player, Ben Ball, from Dallas, coming in from his session with my new South African partner. I waved my racket and called over.

"How'd you do, Ben?"

He looked a little rueful. "Five and six."

I was surprised. "Gee, that's great." I thought, naturally, he meant games.

"Points," he responded, and looked even more crestfallen. Russell had done it again.

Our first round doubles match put us up against a pretty good pair of players. The day was perfect. Blue sky, just a little hot, and no measurable wind. After some small talk, from which Russell abstained, we got down to business. It wasn't easy, but we took the first set Six-Love, after both of us had made some clean hits. The score reached Five-Love in the second set, and although we were down 40-30 for the game I was already counting the spoils of the victor. Then Russell, who had been playing in the forehand court, came over to me. Carefully turning his back to our opponents, he raised his hand to about the height of his belly button, clinched his fist, and with an intense stare into my eyes, said in his broad-"a" English accent, "Tighten up. Don't let the baastards win this point." Without another word, and with no trace of a smile, he turned and moved back into position.

I was startled by the quickness and force of his action and more than a little upset by his seeming lack of sportsmanship. We had the win cinched, so the least we could do was give them a game or two. I was still thinking about it when the ball came zapping over the net in the best serve the other side had made all day. By the time I got my mind back in the game they'd scored because of a sorry return I'd have been better off not even hitting.

In a way, that one point turned my game around for good. And Russell has never let me forget about the time I let the other side chalk up a score.

MENTAL TOUGHNESS

A lot of good players don't win. They have all the strokes but lack the one vital ingredient which is no respecter of age. They don't have what is called mental toughness.

Mental toughness is concentration on the job at hand, the ability to bear down and demand more of your body at the very moment you feel most tired, and a number of other things. It's not a difficult concept to understand but it's hard to learn. Once mastered, though, it will make the difference between winning and losing.

People who play tennis, from the couples who indulge in weekend-only mixed doubles to tournament level singles players, all, no matter what they say, have a better time when they win than when they lose. Since we all play for enjoyment, it follows: Because there is more enjoyment in winning than in being second, you should play to win.

IF YOU CAN, YOU OUGHT TO

More to the point is the basic philosophy which says if you can beat an opponent Love-Love, you ought to. It is a disservice to yourself, the person you're competing against, and the game to play and not give your all in every match.

Many people feel it's not very gallant to sweep game, set, and match without allowing a single score by your opponent. But consider the alternatives: First, if you're serious about playing, you have to break your own concentration to "give away" a point or two. Breaking concentration is a bad habit. It will cost games in the future. Second, to give away those points, you don't have to work as hard. Or try as hard. Functioning at any level less than your best will reduce your best. Finally, your opponent deserves to leave the contest with a fair measure of his skill and yours.

An inflated idea of ability, gained by your handing over points, isn't going to help his tomorrow. In fact, it can provide lazy players with a false impression of their skill and progress.

Giving your total attention and effort to every point in every game, no matter how far ahead or behind you find yourself, has another advantage. Players talk. They talk about games they have played and their opponents. If you never let up and hustle every single point as if it were the last you'll ever be able to score, word will get around. You'll become known as a tough competitor. Not rough, but rugged—the type player who is dangerous in any situation, including contests with people deemed better than you are.

A psychological advantage comes with such a reputation. The player who beats opponents Love-Love goes into a match with the individual on the other side of the net already assuming, in many cases, a mental attitude which hinders full concentration. Concern about getting one point instead of winning the game causes worry and carelessness. No one can win if he is worried and careless.

Concentration, then, is a key ingredient to victory. The ability to concentrate is natural and everyone has it to a certain degree. Top athletes, in addition to physical strength, reflexes, and eyesight, have exceptional talent in this area.

YOU CAN IMPROVE YOUR CONCENTRATION

All of us are able to take our present level of concentration and expand it. Age is no barrier. In fact, the older player may have an advantage here over the younger enthusiast because of greater mental stability. The experienced player, who no longer has to worry about how to hit, can center his or her mind on where to hit to do the most good. Both intermediate and advanced players, especially the older players, know their strokes. What they need to be more effective is better concentration and a solid game plan.

DEVELOP "MUSCLE MEMORY"

Concentration is important to new players as well. They will learn quicker and improve faster by concentrating on the development of a "muscle memory," which will pave the way from worrying about "how" the ball is stroked to analyzing "where" it needs to land in play.

Many professionals don't teach this skill. Some of them understand it, but they tend to have a hard time passing it along. Yet it should be taught from the very first time a new player walks onto a court. There have been many drills published to develop proficiency in swing and style, but no one has put together a program to increase a player's mental toughness, focusing on thought and allowing the swing to groove itself along natural lines.

Tennis is a very psychological game. To be able to get into the proper mental state, you have to pay the price of admission. You have to be in reasonably good physical condition, be willing to practice to gain, then hold your muscle memory so you can hit the ball, and be able to concentrate. Concentrating players operate two to three shots ahead of the ball in play. Some carry on elaborate silent monologues which run something like this: "I hit a deep cross-court, then come to the net. He hits down the line. I cut it off with a cross-court volley. He'll be forced to lob." And so it goes. Each time a shot is made, another moves into the possible list of responses, and the concentrating player alters the plan of the game on the spot. He has focused his attention and is not simply responding to the opponent's shots.

START BEFORE YOU START

Concentration starts before the game does. In a tournament, for instance, it begins during practice. Watching how your opponent plays while warming up can provide an amazing amount of information about style, weaknesses, strengths, idiosyncrasies, preferences, and problems. It's more than worthwhile to arrive early, get yourself ready to play by having a private warm-up before you go to the court, then spend the time normally required to "hit a few" in returning the ball in a variety of ways to determine how your opposition responds. Your observations can prove valuable as the game proceeds.

Likewise, if you have the opportunity, watching another player in a match can give you several effective bits of information about his technique. Concentrating on building a mental catalog of strong and weak points will result in a decided advantage when you finally play.

LEARN TO CONCENTRATE WHEN YOU PRACTICE

Concentration also comes into force when you spend time in practice with a friend, as opposed to playing a scoring game. The trick is to stay on the court only as long as you are able to concentrate on each ball, allowing your swing to come from muscle memory. At the first sign of a wandering mind, it's time to take a break or quit, because from this point on, until you refocus your attention on the ball, all you will be developing is a bad mental habit. You might use these sessions to work on shots you don't do well. Repeating a stroke you are already able to handle time after time with no game pressure will result in overworking your muscle memory and learning to mis-hit what you have already mastered.

BECOME A BALL WATCHER

During these same low-pressure training periods, it's a good idea to work on ball watching. Few players are good enough to see the tennis ball actually leave their own strings, but most, even if they wear glasses, can see it come off the other player's racket. When it leaves and you have eye contact with it, you get a little more time to position yourself for the return. Watching it from the very start of the stroke causes you to get your racket back faster and set yourself in a more precise location.

DEVELOP A TECHNIQUE FOR CONCENTRATION

Concentration can be practiced alone, as well. As simple an exercise as bouncing a ball on the face of the racket, trying each time to make it go just an inch higher while you exclude everything from your mind, except the flight of the ball and the force of your next hit, can be used to cause deeper and deeper mental control.

It's hard to imagine how many times an experienced player has seen a person slamming a ball against a backboard again and again in a listless, dull repetition. The same workout, with the added factor of concentration, can be worth points in a game. Concentration is the vital addition to every drill.

People concentrate in different ways. Some are highly animated. Between points they pace and talk to themselves. Others are outwardly icy cold, carrying on dialogues inside their heads. Some are bothered by noises alongside the court, and in fact use these to bring their attention back to the play. Others don't hear anything outside the boundary line, devoting full attention to the ball and the opponent. These techniques work because they achieve the same thing. Full concentration on the action is required for the development of plans for every possible contingency and advantage.

LEVELS OF CONCENTRATION

Concentration increases as playing ability improves. If you think of the mind as a sort of information processor, the beginning player has to consciously enter about fifteen things every time a stroke is made. The more experienced athlete already does most of this as the memory of one whole set of actions, rather than as a collection of items each to be recalled individually, allowing him to explore additional possibilities. Both are concentrating, but one has the ability to bring greater focus against the nuances of play to determine exactly where and what kind of a placement should be attempted next.

CONCENTRATION IN ACTION

Let's follow concentration through several instances on the court. For example, you've just made a solid first service only to have the ball land six inches out of bounds. The threat of double faulting is strong in your mind as all you need is this one point to win.

A number of thoughts should automatically go through your head as you get ready for the next serve: First, you need to evaluate the receiving ability of your opposition carefully. If your hardest shots have been taken consistently, the serve you're about to make, which will be softer because it's imperative you get it in, is going to come back to you with brutal efficiency. Evaluate which returns have been hardest for the other side. If the backhand is weaker, you should go for it. If there is no discernible difference and your opponent is on everything like a demon, your best chance is to send over a ball placed so you have some confidence in predicting where it will be returned.

Watch your swing. There is a tendency to hit too softly. Be firm, but not murderous.

You can also vary your pace. If you've played consistently, a hesitation to alter your timing and a different position from which you serve can disturb the receiver for a vital instant.

Giving your very best at this point is critical. With one ball already gone, you'll be pressured. Thankfully, relief, as the ads say, is just seconds away. Develop a thought-centering, attention-focusing trick. There are many. Bounce the ball and try to catch it without moving your hand up or down. Examine the strings of your racket while setting your mind onto a perfect picture of your serve. Don't rush, in any case, into making the play. Suck in a deep breath and concentrate on slowly letting it out. It's been proven to be an effective release technique to reduce tension.

Take your stance naturally. Don't move about, trying to plant your feet extra firmly, because you run a risk of changing your normal position. Before you start through the motion, think where you want the ball to be when the opposition plays it. Now for the hard part. Block out everything but one simple, positive move—something you are sure to be able to do, like making a smooth toss of the ball. Then go get it. Throw it and focus your mind on where it will land. Watch the ball onto your opponent's court. By this point, your fears should have vanished and your concentration expanded to the point where you are more than ready for a sucessful stroke.

Another instance where concentration can help is when both players are tiring. After an hour or so of ninety-degree heat, it's difficult to keep your mind from wandering into the shower. Often at this point the pace of the game settles into a by-rote repetition. All players fall into routine habits. Observance of this fact can and has scored morale-breaking points. If you see this situation developing, you want to be the one who forces a change, because a sudden sharpening of play intensity will often result in a mistake by your opponent and an almost free game.

It goes back to never letting up. Even the best players have highs and lows during a match, but their low points may be higher than the absolute maximum of many others. The calling forth of an extra effort just at the time when everything has fallen into a doldrum is precisely the right technique. Once mastered it's the key to a dramatic increase in wins.

Even during a blasting by a superior player it's possible to work on your concentration. You can not only watch what your opponent does but try to work out his game plan. It's frustrating not to be able to put your racket onto serve after burning serve, but getting mad and giving up won't help you return it. Instead, try to find a pattern in the other player's placement, to allow you a vital split second to get onto the ball. By watching and concentrating you may see your opponent begin to ease off. It's possible a good hit can upset your competitor's mental equilibrium and cause a letup for the next few points. You may not win, but you won't get killed either.

CONCENTRATION HELPS YOU BE CONSISTENT

Concentration on the game is vital if you are to play consistently. An individual who always seems to have his shots working is a concentrating player. Those who go from very-good and sometimes-almost-great days or plays to periods of mediocre tennis should look first to their ability to focus on the game in progress. Because they play well on some days, it is obvious they have the strokes. What these players lack is the ability to be constant in their concentration.

NULLIFY THE NEGATIVE

Mental toughness is, however, more than just concentration. It is composed of two parts strong ability to concentrate and one part physical stamina which can be called on to provide the extra effort at the right moment. The only other ingredient is the ability to ban all negative thoughts before and during a match. If you go into play psyched up about your opponent and not certain you can win (or worse, certain you can't) you're in a poor position from the first serve on. If, on the other hand, you set out with a positive attitude, even when facing superior opposition, you might not triumph, but you'll be able to score more points, give the other player a harder time, and have more fun yourself. Knowing you played your best against someone who is better has to give you more satisfaction than taking a drubbing.

FIGHT WITHOUT LETUP

Few people understand mental toughness and fewer still realize it can be developed, over a period of time, like any other tennis skill. It's a little harder to work on than a forehand return, but it can be practiced. Hitting only as long as you can concentrate fully on the ball and the play situation is a good start. With training, the periods of full attention can be expanded. The time between points and serves is used to refix concentration and plan a newer, more updated game strategy, based on the ongoing observations of the opponent's play. Game by game, you can bring yourself into the same mental condition as the winning player. Each point, every shot, and therefore the match can be fought without letup. Ahead or behind, you will be able to bring your game into play with force and precision. It's hard to beat.

DON'T COMPOSE HEADLINES UNTIL AFTER YOU WIN

Before learning about the necessity of mental toughness, Jason was playing Budge Patty, an ex-Wimbledon champion, in a singles match in Marbella, Spain. The first points went well for Morton and it was a great day for tennis. The blue Mediterranean and the arid, green-brown, semitropical vegetation gave the occasion a romantic, foreign flair. Before he knew it, Jason had run up Four-Love in the first set. Secure, he allowed his mind to drift: first to the scenery, then to what the newspapers would say later—a headline, something like, "Morton Kills Patty Love-Love." When his attention came back to the game, he was down 5-4. Composing headlines put him into a tight spot and he had to refocus on the game and play like hell to win 7-5, 6-2.

WHAT AM I DOING OUT HERE?

Presently there is only a small percentage of players who understand and use the principle of mental toughness. Those who are able to think positively, focus on the game, plan their shots ahead of time, and put out an extra effort when it's needed are in a position to win many matches from opponents with better hitting ability. These traits are usually found in abundance in the older player. There are a number of reasons for this, but youthful impatience is probably the key factor.

Mental toughness plays a role in keeping you from losing by simply quitting. Tennis players are alone in their minds, even when playing doubles. It's easy to dump a match. There are numerous ways to lose so no one will ever realize you didn't give your best. During a long, hard set, especially on a very hot or cold day, every player, sooner or later, will ask, "What am I doing out here?" The physical fatigue exhibited by a pounding heart has set more than one senior player wondering about matters of health and common sense, especially when you reach the age when college classmates' names start showing up in the obituary columns. The number of excuses which can run unbridled through a player's head at this point is countless. A toe hurts and it's a blister forming. Your right arm twinges and it's the start of tennis elbow. A stretched back muscle produces a pain in the chest and it's the beginning of a heart attack. Almost anything can break concentration and make you let up, if you allow it to.

YOU'RE THE ONLY ONE WHO KNOWS YOU'RE LETTING DOWN

Some players have the reputation of backing off when they are too hot or too tired. Their opponents, or at least the smart ones, will deliberately play them into this situation whenever possible. Only mental toughness can defeat this reaction and keep you from giving in. You don't have to leave the court physically to lose. The constant thought can cost you the game. Splitting your attention will be enough to make you drop points. Only you know if you are letting down. You are the only one who can guard against letting down. It's habit forming, so catch it before it becomes second nature, control it, and stay on guard for its appearance in the future. Occasionally the feeling will try and make a comeback. You need to be ready to respond.

PUSH BACK TO PUSHERS

Mental toughness is the answer to a number of playing styles most often seen by senior players. For instance, the "moon ballers," known in some parts of the country as "pushers" or "slow ball artists," don't give you a playable ball. They always manage to hit it back because their slow, plodding method of play, with easy returns, never gives you the opportunity to do your stuff. Moon ballers are tough enough to stay in there forever. Or until your impatience and desire to lay one away makes you break concentration and knock it out of bounds.

The game strategy against this aggravating hitter is to stay alert and not to try to work miracles with balls that give you nothing to return. Overreaction will force you to overhit. Deepen your concentration and set your plan. Repace your play to match the moon baller's and hit back easy. Stroke every ball deep into his far court to keep him there. Be patient and stay on it. By keeping him back, you're going to cause him to dink a short one and you can blast or drop shot for the point. Other strategies will work, but only if you concentrate and slow down your play to allow yourself time to build a game plan that will not force you into overreactive mistakes.

A BANGER CAN BE YOUR BEST FRIEND

As vexing as the moon baller might be, the "banger" is worse. Bangers hit for winners only. Every shot is a killer and they press, press, press.

On a good day, and with a little luck, bangers can beat just about anybody. On an average day, which is most of the time, however, they lose. Trying for a kill at every chance will lead to inconsistency, not to mention forcing a player to be more accurate than most pros.

Mental toughness will defeat a banger anytime. First by resisting the tendency to answer every smash with an even hotter return, the player who concentrates and plays his plan will be better able to judge the flight of the ball to determine which ones will fall out of bounds and which should be returned.

A banger can be your best friend. He allows you to set the pace of the match, establish your strategy secure in the knowledge of what he is going to do at almost every turn, and develop a pattern of play which gives him shots he can't resist trying to murder. If you like winning, you'll like finding a banger and outthinking him.

FRUSTRATE THE JUNK BALLER BY CONCENTRATION

The "junk ball" player is another case. In the same way a banger tries to score with every shot, the junk ball expert plays a never-ending series of angles, drop shots, half volley drops, half volley lobs, and other esoteric balls intended to catch you off guard and flat-footed.

In some circles, junk balling passes for thoughtful strategy. What it actually is can best be described by comparing it to attendance at a practical jokers' convention; when you walk in the door, you are already alert. After a couple of scams in which your opponent gimmicks his way through a repertoire of odd tricks and returns, you get ready for anything. You know there's a catch to it so you expect the unexpected.

Junk ballers win a lot of games they shouldn't by frustrating their opposition. Mental toughness will ease this natural reaction and help you turn the tables. Even junk ballers are human and they tend to develop habitual replies to the same stimulation. You hit down the line in the same way to the same spot time after time and they respond. Concentration will establish a predictable pattern. Watching the ball off their racket will give you the extra time you need to anticipate the latest quirk and return it.

Players with these and even more unusual persuasions are to be found in almost every tournament. As a matter of fact, some do pretty well.

But you seldom see them in the finals because somewhere along the way they run into a mentally tough player.

INTENSITY IS THE BEST PSYCH-OUT

One of the funniest techniques to watch in winning tennis is the employment, by an otherwise excellent player, of the "psych-out." A remarkable number of people are capable of psyching their opponents into playing a game far below that which they are capable.

One such situation occurred at the University Club in Houston. Two men of about the same ability were taking their warm-up shots. They hadn't met before, but both knew of the other by name and reputation. After hitting a few balls back and forth, one missed. As he walked to the net to retrieve the balls, he looked over at his foe. Without breaking stride, he shook his head. "Boy," he said in a voice heavy with admiration, "you've got some backhand."

Smiling, pleased, the other player came forward.

Ready, the first man timed his next line with a preciseness which would have done credit to a professional actor. "Tell me," he said sincerely, "do you take a breath on your backswing or before you start it?" Bouncing the yellow ball casually, he stood waiting for an answer.

His adversary hesitated, honestly considering the loaded query. It was the beginning of the end. From then on his concentration was split between trying to decide just exactly when it was he did breathe and playing his normal game. The result: a lost match. It came from a masterfully executed ploy.

A lot of psyching goes on in tennis, ranging from compliments like, "I've never seen your forehand so damned good," after a tight point, to "How much water do you drink between sets?" Others, who tend to be more subtle, slow down the play to a maddening pace by constantly tying their shoes, cleaning their glasses, or a hundred other tricks. Some have even been known to make deliberately bad calls early in the game to infuriate their opponents. An angry player seldom does well.

Mental toughness is the only effective response to these tactics. If your concentration is on the game and you are always ready to make a second or even a third effort, nothing will bother you. If you are thinking positively, planning your game, and trying to stay ahead of the ball, you won't have time to doubt yourself. Or be badgered into an angry reaction. No one can successfully psyche out a mentally tough player who is using all available power of concentration on the game. In fact, the intense individual tends to dominate the court and a reverse psyching out takes place.

WANTING TO WIN ISN'T ENOUGH

Many players with a desire to win don't want it badly enough to pay the price. They'll practice and improve their physical skills, but they either don't know about or avoid the single most important ingredient: mental toughness. It can be learned like anything else. And it makes the difference between winning and losing.

Remember! Mental toughness: part concentration, part positive thinking, part never letting down, part never giving up, part second and third physical effort at the time it's needed. It may sound like a grade B movie pep talk in a college locker room before the big game, but it positively is the leveling force between younger and older players. It is one sure way to walk off the court a winner more often.

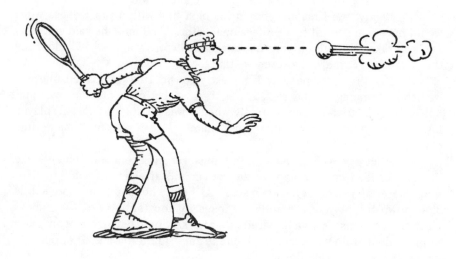

SUGGESTED DRILL

Almost every tennis drill from bouncing the ball on the face of the racket to an elaborate sequence of shots and returns with another player can be used to improve your mental toughness.

Recently, psychologists have revealed some interesting methods of improving concentration. It is a learned skill which anyone can develop to a higher level. How? By really concentrating on something. It's a learning-by-doing process.

Take a simple situation in which you are rallying with another player. Without increasing the speed or hardness of your stroke, concentrate on watching the ball leave the other hitter's racket. Follow its path through the air and try to see it impact with your swing. Anticipate where the ball will end up and focus your attention on its flight.

Watch your opponent hit it back. Keep this up without allowing another thought to interfere with the process. Continue as long as you can exclude your surroundings, the background, everything but the flight of the ball and its impact. The second your concentration is broken, stop play. Don't even try to return the hit. Just stop. Right then determine why your mind wandered. If you can identify a reason, note it, take a little walk around in a small circle, take a couple of deep breaths, and then when you are relaxed again, repeat the exercise.

The concentration will get you ready to return the shot quicker and easier. And the exercise will tire you mentally. Keep at it in a single practice until your periods of absolute concentration begin to grow noticeably shorter. Then quit for the day. Go ahead and play if you like, but don't do any more drills until you've had the opportunity to rest.

During the game itself, hold your attention to the business at hand. Don't chitchat, ponder the score, or mess around with a thousand other things. Be civil, but play tennis. Concentrate on the ball, your opponent, and the building of a game plan beyond the play taking place at the moment.

If you'll try it and work at increasing your ability, the improvement will show.

As for the physical side of mental toughness, see the chapters on warming up, cooling down, and fitness. They'll provide you with more than enough tips on conditioning to carry you through normal—and most abnormal—situations.

5
Tournament Competition

"When tennis players get together, they talk about tennis. And about tournaments they've played. Someone always asks, 'How'd you do?' It's great to be able to answer, 'I won it.'"   Jason Morton and Russell Seymour

It had rained the night before, so it smelled fresh. The grass courts in Philadelphia had a wet, green shine in the brilliant morning sun. Grass is a tricky playing surface even when dry. A little dampness makes it even more unpredictable. Balls take a funny bounce and there is a little slipping motion between the shoe sole and the ground.

"It doesn't take much water," Jason said, as the two men walked out of the locker room for the finals of the 1978 Grass Court Over Forty-five Doubles Championship. "You can spit and wet it down enough to make it as slippery as a greased hog."

Russell nodded, saving his comments for the game. He was in a state of intense concentration.

The two walked along the red brick pathway to the main arena where they paused at the edge of the tight, neatly trimmed, white-lined court. Clouds were obscuring the sun but they separated allowing a sharp light to fall on the almost glowing-green surface.

Jason stepped across the boundary marker to test the grass tentatively by sliding his foot back and forth. "It's bad, but it'll dry some before we start."

Russell broke his silence. "It had better. Or we'll need bloody water wings to get about."

Side by side, they continued on to the players' ready room.

The threat of rain did little to dampen the enthusiasm of the crowd which gathered to watch the finals. The tournament, now in its sixth and final day, had pulled well. Enthusiasts had been on hand for every match and had been rewarded by being able to see some fine play.

Especially good were Bill Lust and John Powless. Playing tight tennis plus exercising good judgment and teamwork, they had beaten all comers to forge their way into the finals. It was their big chance to break the Morton-Seymour stranglehold on the title and they were ready. They had played remarkably well in the semis and managed to rout pair after pair of rivals.

The onlookers waited, casting careful eyes at the light gray clouds floating in the otherwise blue sky. There was a feeling of tension, shared by players and watchers alike.

The match started sharply when Seymour, on his first service, bored the ball over and took the point on a blooping return which failed to clear the net. But Lust, and later Powless, showed equal skill.

As the play continued, Jason and Russell, in keeping with their style, talked quietly to each other between points. Just into the second set Russell turned and nodded. "You were right. That Eastern Grip is making him pull down on his overhead."

"Let's watch it once more to be sure."

On the next exchange the two controlled the play to allow John Powless a smashing overhead. They managed to return it, and after taking the point, conferred again.

"That's it, all right." Tan and athletic, Seymour was looking away from Jason, over the white net. The sun was brightly burning away the clouds.

Jason squinted as he assumed his stance. His voice was low so as not to carry to the other side. "You want to use it now?"

"Let's save it. We're getting some damned odd hops on the ball, and they are hitting very well. We may need the ace."

The play was evenly matched. Both teams were moving well, working in tight unison, hitting with astonishing accuracy. The individual games were long because both sides made no mistakes and were able to return almost impossible shots. The pace of the action was fast with first one side then the other taking the lead.

At last it came down to the crucial moment. Emerging equal after a resounding final set, they were forced into a tie breaker. It was win or lose, with the winning team the champions.

After the first point, Russell dug the toe of his shoe into the still-damp grass. He was breathing a little heavily but there was no other outward sign of tension or tiredness.

"It's now or never, mate. Let's give him some lobs to hammer back and see if he cracks under the strain."

"Okay, but keep him back there deep."

Again using strategy, Russell maneuvered the play toward Powless. A long, high, very deep lob moved John back into the far corner of his court. He met the ball with a powerful overhead, smashing it back at Jason, who managed to pick it off. The ball had cleared the net by a couple of inches, due to a downward force being applied to it at some point in the swing. The tie breaker remained even, with both teams holding on.

The crowd was hushed as the men took their places. This one, final point would end the affair by crowning one team national grass court champs.

Lust served to Jason, who returned it with a small amount of spin, hoping for a crazy bounce on the slick surface.

"Let's try his overhead again," Russell urged. Jason nodded in agreement.

The opportunity came on the next shot. The lob went deep and Powless moved to meet it. He started into the smooth motion of his overhead, hitting the ball cleanly. But a combination of tension, tiredness, and grip added to the downward deflection. The ball snapped forward, only to be stopped by the net.

Jason and Russell were the winners for the third consecutive year.

HOLD SECRET WEAPONS UNTIL YOU NEED THEM

The art and science of playing effectively in a tournament takes time to learn. Sizing up an opponent's style and potential weaknesses is a basic skill of any good competitor.

The more exacting challenge of when and how to use this knowledge is a little harder to master. But once understood it will give any observant player an "ace in the hole."

Many people, when they find a weakness or lack in an opponent, force the play to concentrate on the problem area too soon and for too long a time. They give the other person enough practice to cure the shortcoming by going to the revealed difficulty over and over. Then, when they need a crucial point, they don't have a secret weapon.

Tournament players with experience avoid this error. They know every game can come down to one or possibly two critical points. They wait, sometimes impatiently, for the right instant, then like judo experts, turn the fault into their own success.

STAYING COMPETITIVE IN TOURNAMENTS

Tournament play differs from ordinary day-to-day playing in a number of ways, due mostly to the added level of tension and excitement.

Even in a club tournament the pressure on players mounts as they play set after set, moving closer to the semis and finals. Spectators add to this feeling even when the gallery is made up of other competitors.

Many good players do well in the early stages of an event, but fail to stay competitive toward the end where it really counts. They allow the overall activity to awe them or they fall victim to thoughts such as, "I've had to win my last five sets. I don't know how much longer this can go on." The implication that the law of averages is at work has little basis in reality but some people seem to think this way.

Another difference in tournament play is centered on the fact you are allowed no losses. It's a winner-take-all deal. In order for you to be the tournament champion, you have to win every match. One defeat and you're done.

HOW CAN YOU REMAIN AT YOUR BEST?

These factors all work together to place an extra strain on every entrant. Some respond positively, using the added stress to enhance their game and outlook. "I never feel so alive and alert as when I'm doing well in a tournament and we're getting down to the end. Everything seems sharper to me so I respond better," is the way one player at a senior national put it. In his case, the stress seemed to work to clear his mind, allowing him to get better as the event progressed. But this reaction is rare. Most people, excited by the forces at work, end up playing less than their best at the exact moment they need to excel.

Mental toughness is the answer. By concentrating on the ball, blocking out the surrounding distractions, you'll find the added stimulation of the crowds, the need to win, and the excitement of the day do make you sharper. But only so long as you are able to focus your mind fully on the play in progress.

We'll come back to the application of mental toughness later, after considering some primary facts about tournaments and the people who win them.

BECOME ONE OF THE TIGERS

Most tournament entrants are social players who have entered an event. Out of a typical field of sixty or so contestants there are probably about eight or ten who have enough of the tiger in them to make it to the semis and finals. There are usually another dozen present who have the playing skills to make it all the way but lack a winning attitude, so they fall out midway. The rest of the entrants, say forty of the original sixty, are just along for the ride. They know they can't play well enough to win, and they won't devote a sufficient portion of their lives working at their game to move up into the ranks of the better finishers.

Why do they come? Because they enjoy it. It's a chance for them to get away from their daily routines. Tournaments provide excellent social events. And there is the added excitement of being a part of an organized activity. An importance is lent to the game, so every individual who participates gains stature. Many back markers play different events because they like to be able to say, "When I was playing in the Southern . . . ," or, "At River Oaks the year I played with . . ." The only difficulty with this conversation is the response, usually not far behind, from even best-meaning friends: "Oh, you played the Southern! How'd you do?" Answering is a little tough when you failed to make the cut after the preliminary matches.

IT'S FUN TO WIN MORE

No matter where in the entrant-mix you might fall, from the not-a-chance pack to the few with the potential to make it to the finals, you can do better in a tournament situation. Even without improving your physical standard of play you can compete harder and beat more opponents. It's all in your head and you will start generating the proper attitude as soon as you admit it's more fun to win than to lose.

No amount of mental concentration will make up for vast differences in players' ability. But if the skills of the two competitors are anywhere near being equal, the right mental attitude will give you an unbeatable edge.

DEVELOP YOUR ALERTNESS IN ADVANCE

Mental toughness starts even before the first serve. Tournaments provide an excellent situation for upsetting potential opponents' minds days or even weeks before they start. Russell, for instance, was called by an acquaintance the week before a senior event. After talking about the forthcoming action, Russell confirmed both he and Jason would be present, playing in the singles, then together in the doubles. This was apparently the information the caller wanted. He'd heard they were going to be there and recognized a formidable combination. Just as he was about to hang up, Russell threw in this blast: "Who did you say you were playing with?" There was a pause, then a name. "Right. Shame. As good a player as you are and all. You've got a dog, there. Afraid you'll never carry him." The combined inference of one player's great skill and the partner's lack of it helped produce an unsettled doubles team and effectively removed them from competition for the top place.

BELIEVE YOU CAN WIN

Russell does this naturally. His level of mental toughness is so great he is always alert for any opening. None of this is intended to imply a lack of sportsmanship, because few love the game as much as Russell does or have given of themselves to help other players to the extent he has. But he likes to be a winner and he knows the importance of the proper attitude.

Getting yourself psyched up for the event is as vital as having the mental toughness to turn the excitement, confusion, and tension to your playing advantage. If you can thrust doubt into the minds of your opponents, so much the better. Even if they only dwell on the matter momentarily, it's an edge. Especially if that moment occurs at a crucial point in the final game.

As we have seen, many players go to tournaments wanting to win, but lacking faith in the idea they can win. They have the desire but not the ability to convince themselves they are capable of the ultimate achievement.

BE A FACTOR IN THE FINALS

This process starts before you leave home. Winning players know they are a force and will be a factor in the finals. Their attitudes, while not openly important or braggadocian, reflect calm sureness. It's amazing the effect quiet self-assurance has on a number of players. It is particularly demoralizing to those who are uncertain of their chances. Many times when an unsure player is paired against a self-assured opponent there will even be pregame apologies. The doubting individual usually instigates the conversation with the remarks like this: "Look, I know I'm out of my water playing against you. I just want to hit a few good returns." As honest as such an appraisal might be, it is surely a long way from a winding attitude.

WATCH OUT FOR SANDBAGGERS

The experienced tournament player also knows to watch out for the sandbagger. The same apparent lack of sureness might be a masterful cover to induce overconfidence in an opponent to cause a slow start. Once in the lead, the person who "only wanted to make a few good returns" shows his true personality by aggressively going for the win. More than one seeded player has been flattered into early game incompetence.

When the play has actually started many people feel a letdown. They have managed to psyche themselves up for the event, have maintained their outward calmness, and are ready to play. Serving the first ball is an anticlimax. All the practice, arrangements, plans, in some cases long distance travel, and the problems of taking part in the contest, things which may have become ends in themselves, are over. The start of play instigates another sequence of events for certain individuals. Right at the moment they need to be their sharpest they face a psychological letdown.

THE REAL BATTLE IS ON THE COURT

Mental toughness is the only way to solve this problem. From the instant you step onto the court you must focus all your attention on the game. The ball, your opponents, position, strategy, all these, must fill your mind, blocking other stimulation.

There is one cardinal rule for tournament play. It's true for every friendly set you find yourself in as well, but it is doubly so for formal games.

The point is not over until it is won.

DON'T LET UP FOR A SINGLE POINT

Someone is going to win each point. No matter how far you feel you might have your opponent in the hole, you cannot afford to back off or let down until you take the score. We've seen this happen hundreds of times. A good player gets the opponent off-balance, chasing right, then left again, barely able each time to make a return, much less place it so as to climb back into contention.

Suddenly, the person with the advantage lets up for an instant. He gets lazy. He hits what looks like sure death right into the opposite corner from where his somewhat-exhausted opponent has just managed to play the last ball. So he takes a second out, standing flat-footed to see what happens. In that instant, his opposition, calling on one final burst of energy, gets the racket on the ball and drills it back. Caught off guard, the player who was on the offensive misses what would have been a simple return if only he'd maintained competitive pressure.

STUDY YOUR COMPETITION

The quality of players who make the middle and end portions of almost any tournament is high. This leads to another interesting situation.

Good players stay ahead of the game by a couple or three strokes. They also have a repertory of dependable shots, some occasional killer tricks, and a few seldom-used specialty plays. By spotting the potentially good players, either by prior reputation or through asking around, you'll be able to arrange to watch your adversary at work on the court. It is hoped he or she will be up against somebody strong enough to make them show a few of their specialty or trick numbers. Careful observation can reveal information about pace, desired court position, and ability to structure the play by making one shot which forcefully leads to a certain return. Armed with this preview, you will be better able to devise a strong game to best combat now-understood abilities.

THINK AHEAD

It's interesting how, after the ball is served, the number of possible responses declines. You hit deep into the backcourt, forcing your opposition, who was beginning to crowd the net a little, to turn and run. He gets to the ball. If he makes it in time to get set, his probable response is a shot down the line. Seeing he can make it, you can already be in motion. Or say your backcourt bomb caught your opponent by surprise. In his race from the net he is a little late in getting his racket on the ball. You see this tardiness and know the return almost has to be a wobbly high lob. You can be moving diagonally in toward the net while the shot is being made, to find yourself in the perfect position for putting away the point almost before your opposition recovers from the previous save.

ANTICIPATE THE RESPONSE

To every action on your part there is a likely counteraction. The more you manage to anticipate, the better your court position will be and the more sure you are of making a clean, well-conceived return. The more thought-out, accurate shots you hit, if you plan ahead at all, the more you force your opponent to give you what you already figured would be a satisfactory response. The more predictable your opposition's returns become, the more you control the game. And the greater your chances of winning.

ACTIVE AND REACTIVE HITTERS

The antithesis of the action-causing player is the reactive hitter. At times this can be effective if the hitter realizes what is going on. There is a technique in boxing called counterpunching. A good counterpuncher, who also has an attack, can beat fighters through secondary response control. They swing at an apparently open jawline. The counterpuncher, ready because it was a setup, anticipates the blow and strikes just after the adversary started to hit. The usual result is the counterpuncher escapes the force of the other fighter's fist and lands a solid return blow. The same thing is true in fencing and other quick hand-eye coordinated sports.

In tennis, a reactive hitter lets you carry the game by only reacting to the strategy you establish. Your opponent relies on your leaving an opening and is ready to capitalize on it.

There are a number of reactive players, but none are champions. No one, in modern tennis and especially in the over-forty game, can give up the advantage of setting both the pace and the number of strokes which will be returned into his strongest plays. In other words, if you are reactive only, you may make some strong opponents nervous, but in the end you'll win damned few matches.

HANG IN THERE EVEN WHEN IT'S ULTRA-TOUGH

Planning ahead is hard to do. It's especially hard to maintain a perspective on the game when the situation becomes ultra-tough. Consider a tie breaker. The tendency to tense up is unavoidable. This usually leads to a more hurried rate of play. Since you are at your best playing at your natural speed, you have a potential disaster in the making. Mental toughness helps here, as does the knowledge your opponent is in no better shape than you are. If you're uptight, so is the opposition. If you can manage to control your impulse for accelerated play and "dance with who brung you," sticking to the shots which have worked so far in the match, you'll be in much better shape.

Another trait to avoid is being a tight-situation, go-for-broke, trick-shot artist. Look at the averages. You're in a tie breaker. That in itself means up to now you've played as well as your opponent. Unforced, self-induced errors can defeat you, but your normal style of play at least gives you an equal opportunity. So don't come down with a case of the crazies and try some half-learned, poorly thought out novelty return.

Play what you know how to play, maintain your concentration, keep the pace as near normal as you are able, and, if you've found a secret fault, try it out. If it doesn't result in your scoring the first time, it's okay to go for it again. But don't repeat the plan for a third sequence or you may end up eating a ball.

BE YOURSELF EVEN IN A TIE BREAKER

You'll know by this point in the game what has been successful in terms of plans and rotation of shots. Do it again. The same plays will work because no one can learn a new style during the tie-breaking set of a championship. Your opponent, too, will be playing his best, most consistent point getters.

If you can manage a little break before the start of the tie breaker, do it. Use the time to fix your full concentration on the ball and your opponent. Try to see yourself in your mind's eye making the shots you know you'll use. Then forget everything else, play, and monitor your own pace. Don't let the other player drag you into a downward spiral of speed.

In doubles, a close rapport with your partner helps overcome the stress, which is why a lot of tournament players do better as a part of a doubles team than alone in a singles match. Doubles is a game of teamwork and angles. Each player supports the other, making the two a single unit on the court. Doubles is not a bad way to start your tournament play, as it will help you, providing your partner is also serious and will maintain concentration, gain mental toughness, and keep your mind on the ball.

LAST SET OPTIONS

Sometimes, in the final points or during a tie breaker, it's a good idea to alter strategy a little. If you've played a number of well-placed shots to the open side of the court and your opposition has managed to get almost everyone, they are showing a consistency of play you can use to your advantage. No matter how you look at it, there are some players who love for you to hit away from them because they are fast enough to make excellent returns. If this happens, change up in the last set. Try hitting behind such a player in the closing moments. Chances are you'll get points because your opponent will have developed a reaction which places the weight on the wrong foot. The little extra time needed to shift and start off will break timing. It will also stop anticipatory starts, slowing return ability even more.

Service during the crucial periods, such as a tie breaker or the seventh or eighth game, also becomes a little harder. You can deal with the extra pressure by consciously playing only one point at a time and maintaining your earlier style. Full concentration on the ball, paying no heed to feelings which demand you slam it and try to ace one, will work together to allow you to play consistently.

START WELL TO END WELL

In talking about important points in a match we've focused on the end game. Actually, one of the most vital scores is the very first one. If you come out fighting, set your strategy, get it into play, and do your best to gain accurate placement, you'll set a trend for the match. Once established, it's hard for your opponent to break out of the flow you've created. Being able to gain control in the very early stages will result in your having less strain as the contest proceeds.

Some coaches adhere to the notion every fourth point is the time to put on pressure, an idea which comes from the pivotal nature of this point whenever the score is 15-30 or 30-15. Whoever manages to win the next one either comes back strongly or takes a two-point lead. This sort of thinking fits the percentages but only if it is not used as a device to relax during other points. The way to win any match is to win every point. If you win each one in turn, applying your best play and concentration as you go along, you'll end up on top. Elaborate plans to work harder at certain places in the game can make many players let off at others. A better solution is to play every ball just as hard as you possibly can. If you get into a hole, don't let up. Don't go wild with something ingenious and new, just force yourself to forget about how far behind you are and center your attention on making the next return.

All points are crucial. Each one you win, the nearer you are to taking the game.

Tournament doubles play is much like singles, but there is the additional problem of teamwork, which can place a new dimension into the match. In the chapter on doubles there are several tips on improving this aspect of your tennis. Working together is mandatory, but it can be overdone, resulting in neither partner playing his own game.

PACE YOURSELF FOR ENDURANCE

In a tournament, a good competitor knows how to pace. Understanding the seriousness of a single loss, the average player gets a little uptight and tends to go too hard too early in the meeting. This leaves him, unless he is in good physical condition, a little run-down for the hardest matches. A professional or seasoned tournament contestant has the need to win, but understands the longer he is in the event, the stiffer the competition will become. There is a need for keeping something back. Because no matter how finely tuned you are, you're bound to come up against someone who is in as good shape, physically, or better.

This shouldn't indicate a loss of concentration or not playing to your maximum ability. It simply means proper pacing and not doing any more than you must in order to win.

ANALYSIS CAN SAVE ENERGY

Observation and careful planning will sometimes move you through the early stages of a meeting without your having to resort to an all-out effort. Here is an example of how acute analysis of an opponent can work in your favor, resulting in easier, early wins.

Marty Devlin is a good senior player. He started the game at thirty-five and has worked hard. A sound natural athlete, he came to tennis having already learned about the winning mind and the need for mental toughness. Teamed with Ken Wilson in the 1978 National Senior Over Forty-five Grass Championship Tournament, he came up against Jason and Russell early in the meet. Seymour and Morton were expecting a hard fight in the finals and, although they recognized Devlin and Wilson as good competitors, they felt they could take them without killing themselves and jeopardizing their later match. Watching the two men play, Jason and Russell realized Devlin had a pattern. Quick and able to get his racket on even the hardest serve, he would hit a good return. Then he would rush immediately to the net where he would wait, ready to score on his opponent's next shot.

When they played, Russell applied mental judo to this predictable movement. He used the other man's force. After his serve, he was ready for a good return. When Devlin hit the ball back, Russell would meet it with a little dink shot which would barely clear the net. Devlin would make the return, but his momentum was broken. Russell used his strength and speed against him by hitting back a little blooper which pulled him out of position. The match was over after the first set. Devlin, to his credit, learned from the experience. He became a harder player to beat in following competitions.

WATCH FOR OPPONENT'S WEAKNESSES

Tournament players, at least those who are usually still around toward the end of the event, get to know each other's strong and weak points. They watch the play with ardent fascination, noting any apparent weakness. After a few exchanges, they can begin to predict each other's response to a shot.

Jason plays Bill Lust regularly in the various championships. He knows Lust has a "creaky" forehand. Creaky means the man's arm sometimes makes an actual noise when he swings. Lust knows Jason is aware of his problem and at some time in the match, usually the crucial point, he expects to have his defect used against him. The last time it happened was in a friendly game played as a warm-up for a tournament. Jason forced him into a forehand situation and Lust's arm creaked. When he missed the shot, the two glared over the top of the net, eye to eye, then both broke into gales of laughter. They knew each other so well each could anticipate the other's reaction to the just-played point.

PREDICT BY PROBABILITIES

Experience in seniors' tournaments indicates some interesting probabilities, such as *the player who takes the first set will generally win the match.* Obviously this isn't correct 100 percent of the time, but it's true far more often than not. The winner of the first set, especially if it was taken after a hard contest, feels ahead. The loser, sensing defeat, applies double the effort. The second set, then, due to these attitudinal differences, tends to go to the loser of the first. In the third set, however, the roles seem to change. The winner of the first go-round suddenly becomes more attentive because any security of position has eroded away. On the other hand, the second-set winner, who played hard, lets down a little. It's almost a complete reversal of the previous games. This is so common in tournament play it largely goes unnoticed. And it's a good example of how uneven effort can lose matches.

Playing every match as if it were the most important, but keeping in mind the necessity of having something left for later on, is a key to winning. It will enable you to take the first set, then remain in a strong position to win.

Of course, you will occasionally run up against another player with well-developed mental toughness. Del Sylvia of Tampa, Florida, is such a person. When he gets into a match with someone of equal ability and mental preparedness, you've got a real dogfight. Generalities such as first-set winners usually taking the match don't apply under these conditions.

TRY FOR AN EARLY LEAD

Another interesting and highly observable fact is the advantage which comes to a player who takes an early lead.

Smart players start hard, aiming to gain the first points. This is a powerful tension reducer because it directs the nervous energy always present in a keyed-up player into a specific and beneficial channel. Playing the initial points as if you were behind and needed them to win should be your standard style. If you win, it's relaxing to know you do have a lead, so you can lose a point without costing you the game. The lead lets you experiment a little in the early stages of a match to discover things you might need later if the score tightens up.

An early lead also has a negative effect on your opponent. Eighty to 90 percent of all players falter when their opponent moves into a commanding position of early dominance. In addition, a number of people simply lie down and die after losing a few early points. They give it up or start trying to find excuses for their bad play.

COMING UP FROM BEHIND

The best defense against the early-lead position of power is to have it yourself. But that's not always possible. When you find yourself unable to get moving on your opponent, don't panic and start doing any number of unpracticed and poorly thought out things. Play your game. Settle your mind, concentrate on the ball, hit as easily as you can, and fix your concentration on the point in contention, not what you did or might have done on one already credited to the other side. If you can maintain your game, set the pace for the match, and don't give up, you've got a fine chance to come back.

STARTING HARD

Starting hard is difficult to learn. There is a tension associated with the first serve of a tournament. Players are relieved when the ball is in play.

In their early days of playing doubles together, Jason and Russell had real differences on this basic point of strategy. On several occasions, when facing opponents they felt would not give them too hard a contest, Jason would play the early points easily. His loose hitting would irritate Russell, who cannot stand to slop around. Seymour, who even plays training matches with concentrated intensity, was finally able to convince Jason of the value of an early lead when they found themselves behind in a game they should have won with ease.

The early-lead technique, which means you have to start the first set going for the win, is even more effective in club tournaments. The tendency for the average player to feel beaten and play dead is pronounced. By taking advantage of this lack of mental toughness, you'll be able to win a lot of games.

One of the keys to success at the club level is to do something the other players will not. Physical training is a good example. Many players take up the game for exercise, which tennis provides. But it takes physical stamina to play well enough to win. Chances are, you can improve your game by following the fitness steps outlined in this book. An all-around physical training program, added to your regular practice and playing schedule, six to eight weeks before a tournament, will give you an advantage, especially if the others against whom you are going to play know about your added effort. There is a strong psychological edge in undergoing a preparedness program. You'll be up for the first set, so in many cases your opponent will be a little psyched at your determination. It will be easier for you to go in with a winning frame of mind. And a little harder for your opposition.

DON'T PRESS TOO HARD

One of the most common faults seen during tournaments is pressing. The player loses sight of the patience required to win a point, resulting in trying to nail every shot into a killer return, or hitting harder. The concentration is good, but it's directed toward things he hasn't practiced and is not certain of doing well.

It usually starts when facing an opponent who, on that particular day, is better than you are. A normal reaction is to try and rise to the occasion by raising the level of your game, which is fine if you avoid doing it by changing strokes or going on a power kick.

MAKE FEWER MISTAKES

The way to improve in any match, tournament or otherwise, is to play within your recognized limits, using the shots you know and making them the same way you did during the long hours you spent in practice. The only thing you add is more concentration. In other words, you improve your game by reducing your own errors, not by experimentation or depending upon some unused ability.

There is no good reason, including charity, for you to give an opponent points by making mistakes. Chances are they will have good enough shots to win without your assistance!

Mistakes occur for a number of reasons. The most usual stems from putting pressure on yourself by trying to win points from behind the base line. The great equalizer in tennis is the return. If you concentrate on getting the ball back and play easily through long exchanges, sooner or later someone will make an error. Don't let it be yours, caused by a growing tension and a desire to take the first apparent opportunity to rush to the net. Await your chance. If you continue to make smooth returns, you'll get the right opportunity.

TOURNAMENT DRILL

Let's start with an attitude adjustment. Read Russell's quote below with the understanding he is not joking. It's a simple statement of fact made with the utmost sincerity.

"There is no reason my opponent should win his services. Ever. It's quite feasible to break every time."

Got it? Now go back, read it again, then say it out loud.

Do you believe it? Really believe it?

If you do, your attitude is adjusted. If you don't, you've got to sit down and figure out why. Don't feel you're a good enough player? Then start now taking steps to correct your deficiencies. Find a compatible pro and get after it. Or possibly you feel you're not in good enough shape to go out and play hard. That's easy to fix, too. It's up to you. When you can believe Russell's statement and feel it, you'll be well on your way.

ONE POINT AT A TIME

In this drill, you need a friend to work with you. Instead of hitting the ball back and forth down the line, set up and play a single point. You serve the first one easy into your friend's court and the return is at regular playing speed. After the point is made, don't keep score. Just start again. Either person serves a ball knowing the other can handle it, and the point starts on the return. In addition to teaching you to work a single point at a time, this drill will allow you to try a wide variety of your strokes and move you around the court. You should concentrate on winning the point and on not making mistakes. It sounds simple, but it's good practice.

6
Physical Conditioning for the Extra Effort

"Two of your greatest allies in a tough game or a hard tournament are physical agility and stamina. They become even better, more powerful friends, if your opponents know you are in top physical shape.
Russell Seymour

It was 10:30 P.M. and the newscaster on the local channel had just signed off for the night. Neither of the two men in the motel room was tired, but both knew they were facing a hard day which would start early next morning.

The two were known to each other, but had only met a few hours before. They had agreed to share accommodations for the tournament because they were playing doubles together and wanted the time to get to know more about their mutual mental attitudes, their possible strengths as a team, and their ability to work in unison.

They had talked tennis since shaking hands about 11:00 A.M., not stopping during lunch or dinner. Now, with each satisfied the other would make a good teammate, they were ready for bed.

Jason clicked off his lamp, rolled over, and stared at the dim ceiling. "G'night, Russell. See you in the morning."

The reply was muffled. "Night, Jason."

Somehow the answer sounded strange. Jason turned in the narrow bed, raising himself up onto one elbow. What had started as a casual look became a stare of surprise.

The other man was lying on his back in a relaxed posture. His right arm was extended straight up in the air and his forefinger pointed 90 degrees to his hand. In what little light there was in the room, Jason could see Russell Seymour's eyes methodically following the moving finger from side to side.

"Ah, Russell?"

"Right."

"Ah, what are you doing?"

"Me eye exercises."

"Eye exercises? What eye exercises?"

"Me eye exercises I do every night. The eye's a bloomin' muscle, too, you know. Or at least it's controlled by muscles. Makes sense to exercise 'em."

"Ah, right. Exercise 'em." Jason lay back, staring straight ahead. In his mind he was wondering what kind of person he'd chosen as a tennis partner.

About 6:00 A.M. first light came flooding through the narrow windows, bouncing off a wall mirror and reflecting into Jason's sleeping eyes. Irritation from the brightness caused him to screw up his face and roll away from the brilliance. A soft voice dragged him from the last edge of sleep and he was awake, lying still.

The voice continued. ". . . twenty-one, twenty-two, twenty-three, twenty-four, twenty-five. Whew." There was a scuffling sound which seemed to come from the side of his bed. Without moving his head much, Jason realigned his field of vision.

Russell was on the floor in the push-up position. From the look of him, he was about ready to start, but as Jason watched, he rolled over and started doing sit-ups. The counting started again, and Jason realized he'd just missed seeing the last of the twenty-five arm exercises.

"Morning, Russell." Jason's voice was cracked and a little hoarse with first-morning rustiness.

"Morning, Jason." Russell spoke in cadence with his continued sit-up count. ". . . eighteen, nineteen . . ."

"Getting a little exercise, huh?"

"Right. . . . twenty-one, twenty-two . . ."

"You don't let much get in the way of your routine, do you?"

". . . twenty-five." The man on the floor straightened his legs and started doing an exaggerated split, feet clear of the green shag rug. ". . . five, six, . . . try not to, . . . eight, nine . . ."

Jason rolled back over and looked at the ceiling.

Suddenly, from the position between the two beds, Russell sprang up. For the first time, Jason noticed he was dressed in a blue shirt and white tennis shorts. The man looked robust and seemed to bounce across the room to the door.

"Going somewhere?"

"Run me two miles. See you." Without another word, he was gone.

Jason lay in bed for several minutes. He could taste the last dregs of the scotch he'd drunk the night before as a tang at the back of his throat. Lord God, he thought, what have I let myself in for? He rolled to his feet and started for the bathroom. It was going to be a very long day indeed.

SHAPE UP TO WIN

Many people take up the game of tennis to help them get in shape. It's true tennis is a sport requiring skill and agility and it does provide good exercise. Dr. Kenneth H. Cooper in his book *Aerobics*, in which he sets forth a "point" system for various activities to rate their contribution to physical conditioning, gives one set of tennis or twenty minutes of singles play 1.5 points. An hour of tennis will burn 420 calories in the average person, which means if you could hold your diet steady and play eight hours a week you'd expend enough calories to equal around a pound of weight loss.

Playing tennis to get into shape is backward thinking. Any serious player will tell you getting into shape in order to play tennis will win a lot more games.

Tennis, while causing you to be active, is not thought by most experts to be beneficial to your cardiovascular system. For such development, the consensus seems to favor long periods of steady exertion (jogging at a ten-minute-mile pace for instance) as opposed to the start-and-stop effort caused by the tempo of a game. So even though you might realize a weight loss from playing regularly, you still need some additional exercise to work out your body systems completely.

For the club player, and especially for those past forty, the quickest, simplest way to win more games more often is to go on a training program, improve your physical condition to a point above that held by most Americans, and lose a few pounds of body weight.

A hard-played tennis match takes a great deal out of every player, demanding mental and physical activity. Sometime during the match, average players begin to "run down." The strain of the game, the stress on their bodies and the incessant need to think ahead tires them. Without their realizing it, a letup starts. Instead of planning ahead two or three shots, they begin to react, and lose the ability to lead their opponent and start hitting back any way they can. Instead of putting out the extra effort to chase a shot they would have made in the early stages, they listlessly watch as the ball falls just out of reach, in bounds.

If, through improved physical conditioning, you can hold off reaching this point, and your opponent gets there in the final sets, your chances of winning are improved.

More active players would put forth the effort to improve their physical condition if it weren't for one thing. Most people feel getting into shape is an ordeal, and a painful one at that. Some exercises hurt, especially if you are striving to develop a set of muscles to their utmost. But a program designed to get you into better shape than the average club player by strengthening key muscle groups used in playing tennis, and at the same time improve your "wind" or the ability of your body to take in and consume oxygen, does not have to consist of arduous exercises repeated monotonously.

Stronger muscles along with better systemic intake and use of oxygen are easily acquired. By following a regular program, you can notice improvements in as brief a period as two weeks, progress in a month, and have reached a satisfactory above-average level in forty-five to ninety days. Again, remember we're not talking about training for the Olympics or a fifteen-round World's Championship boxing match. We're discussing a level of fitness which will give you an edge over the normal club player. If you're looking for more, say a state of conditioning to compete at an advantage with people who play in national tournaments, you'll have to go farther. If you're that competitive, chances are you won't mind the extra exertion, but it's not necessary to embark on a demanding exercise program in order to reach a reasonable level of conditioning.

Recent studies have shown there are psychological factors that have influenced the attitudes of Americans toward exercise. These range from experiences in the so-called physical education classes in junior and senior high schools to coaches who use push-ups or running laps as punishment for minor infractions of the routine in their training programs. If you're over forty, your attitudinal bias toward exercise may be to think of it as at best dull and at worst painful.

TAKE A SHOW-ME ATTITUDE

As a tennis player, the chances are you're already in somewhat better shape than most of the people in your age group in our society and have a better outlook on athletic participation than they do. A little more effort on your part would make a difference. The way to gain this is twofold. First, if you have a negative attitude toward exercise you need to alter it, so as to allow yourself to enter into a program without being held back by your mind. The plan offered here, which is a minimal routine, will get you in shape, and believe it or not, you won't find it hard to do or painful.

It's important, though, to enter into the effort with the right state of mind. A show-me attitude is fine, and much better than an I-know-I'm-not-going-to-like-this frame of mind. One way to build a more positive thought process is to take up the program and see for yourself.

THEN STICK WITH IT!

The second factor, which is interdependent on your outlook toward exercise, is your ability to start a program and stay with it for an extended time. Tests have shown rather conclusively if individuals can be brought into a routine of physical exercise for several months, they get accustomed to the program and become self-perpetuators of the activity. They form a positive addiction and actually miss the physical output on days when they don't participate. So if you can make yourself start regular workouts and keep on doing them until they are a component of your weekly routine, you'll find they will become a part of your lifestyle and you won't want to give them up. You'll also discover the benefits from full participation—you'll see improvement in other areas as well.

THREE WAYS TO IMPROVE

There are three physical areas on which a player must concentrate. The first is strength in selected muscle groups used in getting to and hitting the ball. The second is the ability to take in oxygen and the capacity of your blood flow system to use it. The third, and in many ways most important, is flexibility.

Tennis is a game which requires large amounts of torso and upper body flexibility. Few shots are made from a standing upright position. Knees are constantly being bent and flexed. Long reaches are made with the arms. Phenomenal amounts of joint movement are required for almost every play.

An individual with good strength and only limited body flex capabilities will be in a bind on the tennis court. The game awards agility combined with strength, but not strength alone.

As each of us ages, a certain amount of our natural ability to bend is lost. No one is certain of the percentage, but some estimates indicate 1 to 2 percent per year past the age of thirty-five is not uncommon.

Fortunately, something can be done. Stretching exercises, specifically designed to increase flexibility, are easy to learn and not hard to do.

Unlike the old strain and bounce movements, these new-generation routines are smooth, flowing into one another. Breathing and breath control, as in yoga, are an integral part of the exercise. Also, like yoga training, each movement is a building block. You do the first to enable you to do the second, and so on.

Faithful following of the exercise routines in this chapter will allow you to reach a sound level of flexibility. There's the trick. By gaining a greater ability to bend, you'll be far ahead of players ten or even twenty years younger who only operate at 50 percent of their attainable peak. In other words, by moving your operational limits closer to your maximum capability, you will outperform many individuals who have greater natural capacity, but who have not worked on getting the most from their inborn ability. All this sounds keen in theory, but will it work in practice? You bet it will. If you'll try it, you can see for yourself.

A SPECIAL WORD TO WOMEN

Another point about exercise that needs mentioning is for women. Time and again women will say they are afraid to work out because they don't want to develop a bunch of unsightly muscles. As an excuse to avoid exercising, it's a great line. As a matter of reality, however, it's pure bunk.

Muscle bulk can be built through exercise. All exercise will develop and increase the size of the muscle being stressed. To get to the bulging, unsightly point, the amount of work required is astounding. Men who pump iron to develop a championship, award-winning physique spend hours every day of the year, month in and month out, doing repetitions of limited-motion exercises with heavy weights. The program outlined here doesn't come anywhere near this point in body development.

The female body will resist the bulging muscle syndrome by itself, because of the makeup of the muscles and the effect of hormones. Women are more rounded, men more angular. Women who engage in a properly designed program don't have to worry about overdevelopment.

The style of exercise also has a direct effect on the conditioning or body building produced. High numbers of repetitions with low or no weights produce muscle tone and good strength without enormous bulk. Fewer numbers of reps with heavy weights develop muscles with more mass. It's possible to gain inches around your waistline from doing sit-ups on a steeply inclined plane. This is usually the exact opposite of why the sit-upper is grunting away in the first place, so there is a scream of frustration when the tape measure shows what was received for all the effort. The sad part is fifty to a hundred sit-ups done three times a week on a flat surface would have had the desired slimming effect and the work required would have been less.

BUILD YOUR STRENGTH GRADUALLY

A muscle is an amazing thing. It takes energy in the form of sugar from the blood, converts it into motion, and performs work. When it becomes over-taxed, it reaches a state in which the blood supply cannot carry off the waste products from the initial conversion rapidly enough. If this continues for a period of time, a soreness results. Muscle stiffness or soreness is a direct sign of overexertion and should be avoided in any program. Not only because of pain (who wants to go around stiff and sore?) but also from the point of return on the exercise investment. Better progress can be made by slowly building repetitions. It is especially true for over-forty athletes because exerting a set of muscles to the point of partial failure can cause you to pull or tear a ligament through an effort to compensate for the weakening muscle group by using an odd angle or turn to bring another group into play for the task.

Another old wives' tale holds it is the last repetition and only the last repetition that does you any good. This is true in bulk muscle building to some extent, but it's a long way from fact in the kind of conditioning needed for tennis. Each repetition, performed in a relaxed fashion, lends to the overall effect and increases flexibility.

EQUIPMENT THAT WILL HELP

Some special equipment is required for performing a few of the optional exercises in a good tennis workout. A weight, which can be held in one hand, is a must. Two to five pounds is enough to start, but eventually you may need ten or possibly even fifteen pounds. Another requirement is a place to do sit-ups. You'll need a pad to go under your butt so you don't rub off the skin near your tailbone, and a strap or something to stick your toes under so you can anchor yourself and get the benefit of the pull-up and let-down. (A partner can hold your feet.)

A quick word about sit-ups, which are an optional part of the plan, is appropriate. It is important enough to mention again in the outline of the program. People do themselves more harm than good in this exercise by trying to perform the sit-up movement with their legs straight. Don't! Unless you're anxious to spend some money with a back specialist trying to cure the pain and strain it will cause. Bend your knees at least ten inches above the surface on which you are lying. Fifteen inches is even better. This protects the back and works the major muscles in the stomach more.

HAVE YOU HAD A CHECKUP LATELY?

Two final thoughts, then we'll outline the program. Many experts recommend a physical examination before a person starts a fitness program. As an over-forty tennis player, you've already been involved in strong physical activity. Chances are you have regular checkups anyway. If you're a newcomer to the sport, it might be a good idea to consult with your physician first. Whether you go as far as having a stress test or not is a matter for your doctor to decide.

A well-known M.D. was once quoted as saying, "The one certain thing I can tell you about a weekend athlete is he is likely to die on the weekend." Strenuous activity, like hard-played tennis, is an effort requiring conditioning. Players should not be so ill advised as to run themselves half to death on the court on Saturday and Sunday, then lead sedentary lives the other five days of the week, drinking and overeating. Don't be a weekend warrior. If you are in this category now, join in the program below and give yourself at least a fighting chance.

NOTES ON DIET

Exercise has a companion on the road to physical fitness. It's called nutrition, and it's probably the most misunderstood necessity in your program to get in shape. A vast wealth of new information in this field shows us what old wise men have already said: "You are what you eat." They might have added, "You perform as you eat."

Even a partial review of the recent findings about efficient, healthful foods for people who engage in athletic events is far beyond the scope of this book. But if you are serious about improving your muscular tone, endurance, flexibility, and other capacities, then you owe it to yourself to look into the growing mass of work.

Research now indicates carbohydrates, the old bugaboo so many diets have been developed to bypass, are to an athlete what gasoline is to a racing engine. The "carbo" is the fuel. So it's no wonder low carbohydrate diets are just exactly what the active tennis player does *not* need.

Almost any public library can provide books on the subject of nutrition. Scan the front pages and reject any copyrighted more than four or five years ago. Things have changed. While you're at it, seek out one with diets for athletic training. You'll be well rewarded for your time.

EXERCISES FOR FITNESS

Here is the series of stretches and exercises which make a whole program. The cartoon diagrams show the main movements. Go through the routine slowly. Do only the number of repetitions indicated for the first three sessions. Then add the number of repetitions indicated by the words "step up." Stay at the new level for six sessions, then step up again.

If you find yourself the least bit sore after the first session, it's a good indication how poor your muscular fitness was. Don't worry, and when the time comes for the next session, the stretching and repetitions will take away the stiffness.

Serious players should do the running routine as well as the general fitness series. We'll talk more about the running at the end of the workout descriptions. Here is the Daily Eleven.

THE DAILY ELEVEN

Exercise 1: Reach for the Sky

Stand up straight, arms by your sides, shoulders back, head erect. Now, moving very slowly, bring your hands up in front of your chest. Take a deep breath as you go through the upward part of this movement. Continue to bring your hands up, slowly breathing in. Hands past your face, over your head, one arm on each side, moving slowly. Higher and higher until you are fully stretched upward. Stretch your fingers to extend them to their maximum. Now continue the movement up by rising on your toes. More and more, rising higher and higher, breathing in as you reach and stretch up. When you hit your maximum upward reach, slowly start letting out your breath and follow the reverse of the pattern you took getting there, to bring you gently back down to the starting position. You should be breathing out all the way back down, flowing the air out at a rate timed to let you end up in your starting stance with your lungs empty. Empty means all the air should be pushed out. You must feel the expulsion of the final few cubic centimeters in your diaphragm. Start with two or three. Step up by one or two. Max out at ten.

Exercise 2: Torso Rotation

Without moving from the position in which you ended after your last upward reaching stretch, turn your toes in slightly toward each other so you're standing in a pigeon-toed way. This keeps the twisting movement from being transferred to your knees, which are meant to operate in a single fore and aft plane, not rotating around in circles. Raise your arms out from your sides, palms down, until they are parallel to the floor. Now, breathing in, twist the upper half of your torso to the left, a half turn. Don't strain. Stop when you feel resistance. When you reach your maximum extension, you should have a lungful of air. Slowly let the air out as you twist around the other way, to the farthest point you can reach on your right. Move slowly, and don't force yourself past the point where it feels comfortable. Your head should follow the motion. Don't rush. Time the breathing so you have a full (and that means really full) breath at one extreme and it's let out at the end of the other direction. Three for starters, one for stepping up, maximum of ten.

Exercise 3: Knee Stretches

When you finish your last twist, end up facing front, standing straight. Realign your toes out from the in angle. Place your hands on your hips. Take a deep breath. Then, while keeping your back straight, eyes front, sit down slowly, bending at the knees. As you go down, let out the air. Move slowly, bending forward over your feet to hold balance. Continue down until your thighs are approximately parallel to the floor. Stop—just for an instant. You should be out of air at this point. Now start straightening up again, still moving slowly. Breathe in as you go up to have a full breath when you are erect and standing again. At first you might find it hard to go down until your thighs are parallel to the floor. Don't go down any farther. The old knee bend which took you clear to the ground can mess up your knees. At least two to start, one for stepping up, maximum of ten.

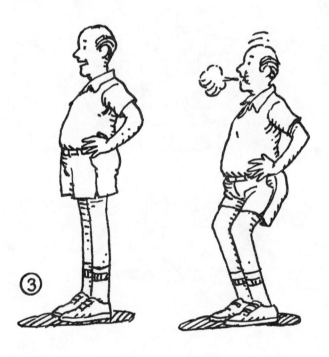

Exercise 4: Bending Torso

Return to the standing position from the knee stretches. Spread your feet twenty to thirty inches apart. Face forward, standing straight. Take a deep breath, then let it out slowly as you bend forward at the waist. Go through the point where your upper body is parallel to the ground. Keep on folding up, like a jackknife, breathing out as you go. Let your arms relax and just hang down. You want to finish up with the top of your head pointing toward the ground. If you have long hair, imagine trying to touch the floor with it. Let your arms dangle. Relax. Now hold the position. You'll feel the pull in the backs of your thighs. Don't move. Stay as you are. Look down. See your fingers near the floor. Don't consciously push yourself. Just imagine your fingertips coming nearer to touching. Slowly but surely, you'll stretch, and your fingers will be nearer. After thirty seconds, straighten up. Again, no fast movements. Breathe in as you come erect. That's once. Beginners should do it twice, step up one at a time, and get to a maximum of ten.

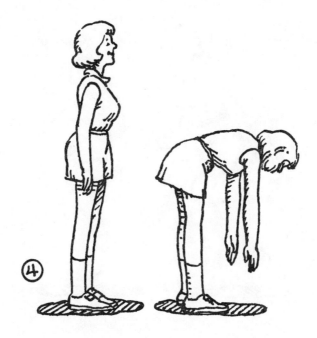

Exercise 5: Leg Squeeze and Hop

When you complete the bending torso flex, you'll end up standing, looking straight ahead. Bring your feet together. Now, for your next move, there are two parts. Balance yourself on your right leg and lift your left foot up by bending your left knee. Reach back with your left hand and grasp your foot over the instep. Press gently, trying to make your left heel touch your upper thigh. Hold this tension. Then, by bending your right knee and springing from your toes lightly, hop up and down on your right foot. Don't come more than a few inches off the ground, but land on your right toe, allowing it to take up the shock. Three hops for starters, two hops each time you step up, ten hops will be enough. Now let go of your left foot, regain your balance facing forward, and do the same hopping series by taking hold of your right foot and springing on your left leg. Same number of repetitions.

Exercise 6: Upper Body Rotation

At this point, you're more than halfway through the Daily Eleven. Not too bad so far, eh? Get your balance back. Face forward, move your feet about a foot or so apart, place your hands on your hips, and take a full breath. Let it out slowly, as you bend forward until your upper body makes a slight angle to the ground. Then, keeping your feet still, slowly rotate in a circle, leaning to the left, continuing the movement toward your back, coming around to your right side, ending up in the bent-forward-at-the-waist position from which you started. Exhale all the way around, and let out the last of your air as you straighten up. Repeat the series, this time moving from right to left. What you are doing is holding your hips steady and making a big circle in the air with your upper body. Move slowly. One to the right and one to the left counts as a repetition. One to start, move up one, and get to five.

Exercise 7: Side Bends

This is like the preceding exercise in that you'll be flexing from the waist again. You end up with your hands on your hips, feet about a foot apart, facing forward. Allow your hands to drop to your sides. Straighten yourself up, standing tall. Take in a breath. Now, starting with your head, and keeping your back straight, lean slowly to your left. As you do so, slide your left hand down along the outside of your leg. Let your right arm go where it will. Concentrate on moving your fingers down your leg, toward your knee. When you touch the top of the first part of your knee joint, start coming back up, sliding your fingers upward until you are standing straight again. Breathe in as you straighten. Don't stop when you are upright. Immediately start the same movement on your right side, moving your right fingers down toward the top of your right knee joint and allowing your left arm to relax. A complete turn is left knee touch, right knee touch. Three for starters, one to grow on, and ten for tops.

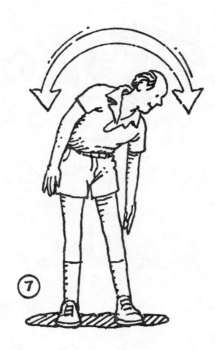

Exercise 8: Arm Extensions

You'll end up from the seventh flexing standing straight, looking forward, feet apart. Fine, hold it. Take a slow breath as you bring your hands up to touch your shoulders. Then, still breathing in, raise your folded arms until the upper arm's underside is parallel to the floor. Now, unfold your arms, straightening them out slowly, still breathing in, until your arms are fully extended. They will be parallel to the ground, and you will look like a "T" with your arms as the cross stroke. Still breathing in slowly, move your head back as you throw out your chest and start lightly forcing your extended arms backward. Bend your hands back at the wrists and, stiff-armed, reach and stretch back as far as you can. Move slowly. Don't force, but stretch. You'll feel it in your shoulders and in the wrists and the arms. Pause. Then breathe out, very slowly, and return to the starting position, standing, arms at sides, facing forward. Three stretches for beginners, add one when you can increase, and get to a maximum of ten.

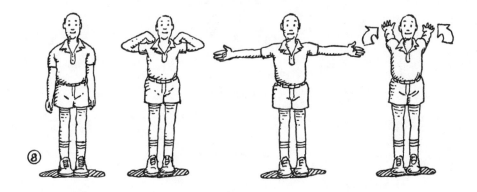

Exercise 9: Shoulder Rolls

When you finish the arm extensions, you'll be still standing upright, legs apart. Let your arms fall to your sides. No special breathing is required for this one. In unison, without moving your upper torso and while keeping your back straight, hunch your shoulders as far forward as they will go. When you reach the maximum, roll them up and forward, as if you were trying to touch the points of your shoulders to your ears. Then, without stopping, continue the motion with a rolling movement on around and try to bring your shoulder blades together, then continue to where you started and stop. The whole movement is a single, slow rotation. After you've done it once in the forward mode, repeat it again starting with the backward thrust, to unwind. One time forward rolling and one time backward rolling make up a set or a rep. Two reps for beginners, step up by one, and max at ten.

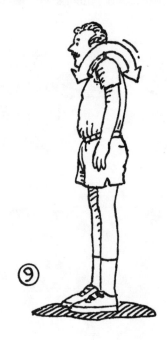

Exercise 10: Neck Twist

You finish standing straight, looking dead ahead, feet apart. Again, there is no breath pattern for this movement. Without moving your upper body, and while keeping your back straight, turn your head slowly so you are looking over your left shoulder. Then carefully, and without exerting much force, continue to turn your head until it is as far as it will go to the left. You should now be seeing things just behind you. Slowly return your head to the front, pause for an instant, then make the same movement to the right. Return to the center and let your head fall forward, trying to allow your chin to rest on your chest. Then, slowly again, lift your head and allow it to go backward as far as you can. The four movements, left to maximum extension, right to maximum extension, forward to maximum extension, and backward for the same, compose a repetition. Three for a start, move up by ones, and ten is a good maximum number.

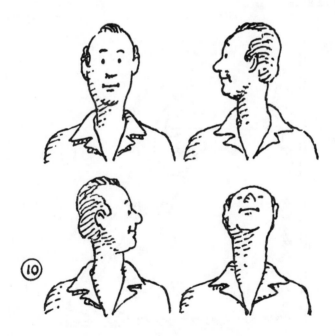

Exercise 11: Leg Stretch

At last, the eleventh and final exercise. For this one, you have to move. It's about time, as you've been in the same spot for a number of minutes. At this point, you've used and stretched every large set of muscles and utilized each major hinge of your body in the proper way. Except for one. The leg muscles got a workout during the one-foot leg squeeze and hops (Exercise 5) but they need a stretch, too. Stand in front of a wall or doorjamb. You should be about two feet away. Put your hands on the surface you are facing and slowly lean forward. Keep your feet flat on the floor and your heels down. Don't go up on your toes. At some point, as your upper body approaches the wall, you'll feel a pulling sensation down the backs of your legs. That's what you're looking for. Don't go so far that it hurts. Just far enough to feel the stretch so you know you're working them. Hold it for a ten count, then push yourself back to a standing position with your arms. That's a rep. Three to start, move up by one, top off at ten.

This exercise program will produce great results and terrific improvement in body flexibility. It's a planned, no-sweat, low-stress routine developed to improve the muscles and joints you use in normal tennis.

It can be done every day or, at a minimum, three times a week. Much study has gone into how often a person should exercise, and most physiologists now agree three times a week, or every other day, is the minimum for a stretching program and the maximum for a heavy-weight, bulk-muscle effort. The day between exercisings allows the muscle groups to regain their strength.

Some people who are presently in good shape may find this initial program too easy and zip through it. That's fine. If you can do it, and do it easily at the maximum suggested reps, you've already got good muscle tone and flexibility. If that's the case, you've probably also got your own workout routine, which is fine too, because if you've gone that far you're already in good enough shape to play winning tennis.

If you find it hard to complete this program, don't worry. Stay with it. You might find you can move up faster than the suggested additional repetitions, but don't push it. There's no reason to. Save your competitive feelings for the court, where you can use them constructively against an opponent, instead of destructively against your own body.

Some people just can't get into the routine of exercise, no matter how hard they try. For many in this situation the addition of a "buddy system" seems to help. All you do is pick a friend who will agree to work out with you. The one prods the other and it makes things easier. This really does work, and you should try it if you're having problems sticking to a training routine.

INCREASED FITNESS EXERCISES

If you want to increase your fitness level beyond the routine already listed, fine. You'll find still more improvement in your game. Here is the next step. It's not as easy, takes a little more time, uses some special equipment, and pays back extra points for every minute you spend doing it.

First, complete the Daily Eleven, which will loosen you up. After you've done the basic exercises, do these in the order following:

Exercise 1: Leg-ups

Lie flat on your back. Slip your hands under your butt to cushion your body from the floor, take a deep breath, and without moving your upper torso, use your stomach muscles to raise your legs into the air until they are ninety degrees to the floor. Keep your knees as straight as possible and breathe out as they go up, and in as you lower them back to the starting position. Start with five, move up to ten, then by steps of three, go to fifty. At this point, you might want to move on upward, but about a hundred will do you all the good you can get from this limited movement.

Because of their physiology, women need to use another motion. From the same position, they should bend their knees, moving their feet toward their body, then, when the knee angle reaches forty-five degrees, slowly straighten their legs until they feel the pull on their abdominal muscles. Hold for a moment, then go back to the starting position.

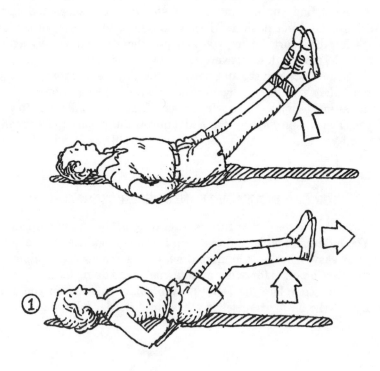

Exercise 2: Curls

This exercise is the one iron pumpers refer to as curls, and there are three different ways to do them. The curling movement uses the biceps and the forearm muscles and strengthens the elbow. Many senior players who turn up with tennis elbow use this series with a five-pound or ten-pound weight and they swear by it. A number of physiologists and M.D.'s also agree it is a useful corrective exercise for the dreaded and painful affliction.

In order to get the full value, three separate motions have to be accomplished. To start, take the weight (five pounds is enough for beginners, ten plenty for the more experienced) and grasp it in your right hand. Kneel down alongside a chair or bend over it so you can rest your elbow on the seat. The weight should be held with the arm cocked, palm of your hand toward your face. Now slowly lower the weight outward and down from your body until your arm is resting on the chair bottom. Then curl it back up again to the starting position. You can also do this exercise standing up, by spreading your feet apart, straightening your back, and holding the weight, palm of your

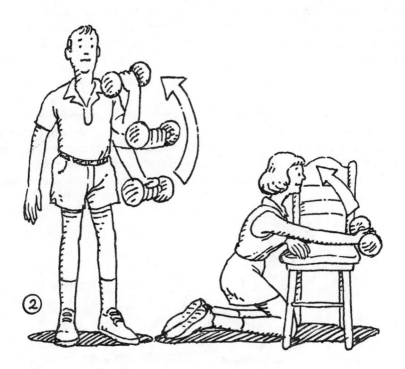

hand forward, by your side. On the count of one, you slowly curl it up to your shoulder, then on two, lower it back down.

Five reps with five pounds, first right-handed, then left, will more than do for a beginner. If you find this too easy, increase the weight to ten pounds. If it's still too easy, double the number of reps. Unless you want to get a well-defined, more bulky bicep, don't move up to a heavier weight, just add repetitions.

The second series is like the first, although you rotate your wrist, so your grip on the weight is palm down. A change in grip uses other muscle groups. The third variation is as the first two, but again the grip is altered. This time, you grip the weight so your little finger and the outside edge of your hand are down. Palms up, palms down, and edge of hand down (the only three ways for you to grab something). Each does its own special work.

One thing needs to be repeated: Take it easy. Concentrate on slow, smooth, precise movements. Do the palms-up series with the right hand, then with the left. Do the palms-down series with the right hand, then with the left. This gives your right arm an opportunity to recover. Then do the palms-up series, again alternating arms so your muscles get a break. You should finish with the edge-of-the-hand-down grip. Remember, you're not going into training to fight someone, so don't overexert. Slowly and smoothly will do more for you.

Exercise 3: Sit-ups

Start with five sit-ups, move up three at a time, and top out about seventy-five or so. Once more, there is a limit to how much good they will do you in a practical game situation. If you're interested in cosmetic results, get a handbook on iron pumping and really get after it. These programs are intended to produce enough fitness to play top tennis, not bring about some

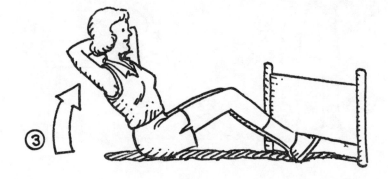

huge weight or size loss from your middle. (In truth, though, if you work up to seventy-five reps, you will gain a noticeably slimmer waistline. It's a not unappreciated side benefit.)

Sit down on a pad. A pillow will do, but a twelve-to-twenty-inch-square of scrap foam rubber is better. Hook your feet under a restraining device (someone, possibly your buddy, can hold them for you), then scoot forward so there is a pronounced bend in your knees. Keep your knees bent at all costs. Now put your hands behind your neck. Lower yourself back smoothly until you are past forty-five degrees from the vertical, then go just a little farther, stop the motion, and return to the sitting position. Let out your breath on the way down and back up, then when you're back where you started, take another lungful of air and go at it again. Don't let your back touch. It's okay for some people to go all the way back, but they don't get much out of the last fifteen or twenty degrees of travel and the risk of pulling a back muscle is far greater than the added benefits. This is a tough exercise. It will do you a lot of good, and it's one you might work on if you want to get into optimum shape. A variation, which helps break the monotony if you work up to seventy-five or a hundred, is to do a regular sit-up the first time, then twist your upper body so you are facing sideways, lower yourself back until your elbow just makes contact with the mat or floor, then return. For the third repetition, twist the other way and touch the other elbow. This works out the large muscles on each side of the body as well.

Exercise 4: Toe Touches

After leg-ups, curls, and sit-ups, it's time for toe touches, which are a great

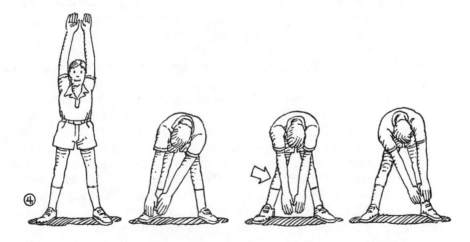

flexibility builder. If you get so you can do them easily, you'll be better off than 90 percent of the over-forties you'll ever see on the courts.

Face forward, spread your feet about twenty-four to thirty inches apart, raise your hands over your head, and slowly bend down at the waist to touch your hands to your left foot. Keeping your hands together, try to touch the ground between your feet, then touch the right foot. Swing your arms and upper body in a circle to the left, straightening up, then leaning back into the movement as you continue it around until you are touching your left foot again. After three, switch the direction of the circle to the right. Do it slowly, don't force, and if you're nowhere near touching your foot or the ground, then stretch a little, but do not strain. In time you'll make it.

It's not necessary for you to do the second workout, but you should do the first series often. You'll find it a little tiring at first, but if you persevere, you'll gain strength and flexibility, and make points you would have lost or considered impossible before you started.

RUN TO WIN

In closing this chapter, a short note on what has been called the best all-around exercise for tennis: running or jogging. The difference between running and jogging is a state of mind. Some people take to this effort easily, enjoy it, and do it regularly. Others find it hateful from the first step, and it never gets any better.

Running, as an exercise, has one strong advantage over all other workouts, aside, possibly, from swimming. It develops your cardiovascular system quickly and efficiently. Your body is able to take in more oxygen, use it better, and your all-important leg muscles get good conditioning.

Even running's biggest supporters in the medical and coaching fields urge moderation unless you are going to become a track star or intend to play big-league tennis.

Dr. Cooper, whom many credit with having started the running craze in our country (and if you don't think it's a craze, go out to your local track some Sunday morning and watch all the overweight, out-of-shape crazies plod by thinking they are doing themselves good), is quoted as saying, "Our most popular program and the one I recommend most is only two miles in twenty minutes four times a week." He goes on to say this is a highly reasonable workout and a vast majority of people can keep it up until they are in their late sixties. He also notes there appears to be little or no additional aerobic gain after running three miles. So unless you are embracing jogging as another sport, it will do you good to run, but you should keep the distance and speed in temperate regions.

If you've never run and are in good health, the run-a-minute, walk-a-minute formula will build up your ability to go a mile, then two, at a steady pace.

You do just what the name implies. You run for a minute, then walk for a minute until the mile is done. Next, you progress to running for two minutes, then walking one. And three minutes, four, five, and so on. By the time you get to running for a solid ten minutes without stopping, you'll have made the mile and be ready to add on the next one-half mile distance.

Don't rush it. Take it easy and watch out for any danger signs, such as a high heart rate, rapid breathing, or clammy skin.

If you're interested in a running program as a part of your tennis training, you ought to buy or borrow any of the many available texts on the subject. A number of popular books on this sport are out and can give you good pointers. One thing, though: If you are going to be jogging or running on a hard surface, such as concrete or asphalt, don't do it in your tennis shoes. As discussed in Chapter 10, these are highly specialized footgear and are not designed to absorb the heel and toe shock encountered in distance jogs on hard surfaces. Invest in a pair of shoes made for running, or in time you'll pay more money for doctor's bills.

Many people who do not like to run find jumping rope a good substitute. A light, springing jump helps build some of the muscles used in tennis. Variations in tempo and style, jumping on first one foot then the other, or crisscrossing the rope in front of your body, add to the difficulty of the exercise and make it fun. If you find running bores you or you just can't seem to get into it, buy a jump rope and give it a try.

7
Warm-ups and Warm-downs

"It doesn't make any sense. In our combined fifty years of coaching and playing, neither of us has known many players who did a warm-up. And the closest thing we've seen anyone do consistently for a warm-down is to go into the club and order a beer." Russell and Jason

Even though Salt Lake City is in a valley, it's still a long way above sea level. Enough so the sky seems bluer and the great gray-black, granite mountains which rim the town stand out in the thin, clear air. The altitude is sufficient to trouble any flatlander who overexerts.

There was no controversy when Salt Lake was selected as the site of the 1977 National Senior Indoor Championships, but no one could have foreseen the dramatic final day.

Jason and Russell were playing each other in the singles events, and together for the doubles. Individually, they had done well, and finally, after days of hard playing, were facing each other on the center court for the title.

They'd gone up against each other before, but on this day, both men came to the arena ready to win.

The match was tense from the first set, which Jason took seven-six. Then Russell, demonstrating his superb self-control, moved into the lead early in the second set. He won 6-4.

The third and deciding series was a killer. The men had been playing for more than two hours without a break. Jason pulled into the lead, had it come even on a call he mentally disagreed with, then faced off for the final

95

points. Jason knew he could win. Looking over the net at his friend and adversary, he thought Russell might be letting down a little. But Seymour called up his reserve of stamina to pull it out. He took the last set, and along with it the match and the championship.

For the entire two hours and forty-five minutes of play, the audience sat enraptured by the fast pace of the game. When it was over, they cheered both contestants equally.

In the showers, Jason and Russell did their best to get ready for the showdown they had coming in less than an hour with Cliff Mayne and Hugh Ditzler, their old doubles adversaries. Both men were breathing hard and knew they had an uphill fight.

The match lasted two hours and twenty minutes. From the start they could see it was clearly going to be a murderous pace. Mayne and Ditzler pulled in front after two games and seized the first set. The psychological advantage was enormous. Ditzler and Mayne gained confidence, forcing Russell to start his "tight spot" pep talk and mental control. Jason joined in, and together they came back to win the second set. But the pace was telling on them. Jason was experiencing the start of leg cramps and Russell took on a steely-eyed look of determination.

The third set came and remained equal. Their old nemesis, the tie breaker, couldn't have come at a worse time. They had been playing tournament tennis at what was for them a high altitude for close to five hours.

Jason served the first two points. He and Russell lost both. The mental strain on them was showing, but Seymour remained consistent. Encouraging, exhorting, concentrating, they made up for the previous loss by taking two back from Cliff Mayne. On Russell's service, they broke even, winning one, losing the other.

Then it was Hugh Ditzler's turn. His big serve would decide the final three points.

Jason's leg cramps were worse, but by stretching between shots he was able to control them.

Ditzler served to Russell, who was unable to make the return. Match point to Mayne and Ditzler.

The next service was to Jason. He managed to get onto the ball, but as it crossed the net, he saw a determined, charging Ditzler come in quick for a hard volley. As Jason started to move to the ball, Russell's sudden shout, "Let it go!" stopped him in midstride. He watched the ball touch down not more than a half inch outside. It was hard to call. There was a long pause, then the linesman's voice came through: "Out."

Russell called for a quick conference. The two perspiring men, breathing heavily, met in the corner of the court away from their still-excited opponents.

"You take the bloody thing, Jason."

"No, you're doing better than I am. You take it."

"Dammit, no. It's yours."

There was a short pause, then Jason nodded. "It's mine."

"And nothing fancy, eh? Just solid tennis."

Jason smiled. "It'll be all I can do to hit it hard enough to get it over the net."

"Remember. Just this one more, then that's it. You can do it."

The two moved into their positions. Jason faced Ditzler, who was determined not to double fault, which caused him to serve at about three-quarter speed. Even so, the ball came like a smoking rocket and it was difficult for Morton to make a clean return.

Hugh Ditzler cut it off, closing to the net, only to have Jason lob it deep, over his head. Ditzler, spinning, moved with astounding speed and got the tip of his racket on it, sending back a low, easy lob, which Russell met coolly. He gave the ball a light tap, and it was over.

Morton and Seymour had taken the doubles, were one and two in the singles, and had played for five hours and five minutes.

Later that same evening, on the return flight to Houston, Jason was eating dinner when the leg which had been cramping in the final points of the match went into a painful muscle spasm. His knee jerked up involuntarily, banging the seat tray, sending salad over the passenger seated next to him. Apologies and explanations made the mess some better, but the people on both sides watched him carefully for the remainder of the journey.

WARM-UPS PREVENT INJURIES

We've seen it, you've seen it, and every other regular player has seen it. What's worse is each of us has done it. Most of us have been lucky, though, and nothing bad has come of it. You get to the court. Not running late or anything. Your opponent or the other three players arrive, you take off your jacket, uncrate your racket, get some balls, then move right out to start hitting warm-ups. How do you do this? With a cold, unstretched body, that's how. You bounce a ball and knock it over or one comes flying through the air at you and you slam it back.

There's only one question: Where's the warm-up? Sure, you might not hit the first ball of the day as hard as you will during a game, but that's hardly a warm-up. The combination of an even mildly extended arm and another eighteen to twenty inches of moving racket go together to produce enormous stress on the shoulder, the elbow, the wrist, and all the bones, tendons, ligaments, and muscles in between.

No reliable records are available but based on a half century or more of teaching and playing experience, it appears more injuries are started and aggravated during what players refer to as their "warm-up" than in actual play. It makes sense this would happen because after you've hit the ball a few times and moved around the court a little, your body is more adjusted to the sudden strains which might be applied to it, so the likelihood of self-damage is dramatically reduced. It's pretty hard to hurt yourself in a game, and when it happens, it's an accident. That's different from inflicting deliberate injury on yourself by starting off cold and striking the ball.

The warm-up is something you may well have gotten along without for years. As far as you know. But as you grow older, the same routines which were traditionally acceptable need reanalysis. It could be you have brought yourself nearer and nearer to injury each time you take the court without warm-up preparation, and you've never quite placed enough stress on yourself to cause it to show. All players after the age of thirty-five or forty should spend at least three to four minutes in a series of preparatory exercises before hitting the first ball of the day. Younger players need to do it, too, but most of them won't. Once again, seniors have or should have better sense, so they can be counted on to take the little time necessary to start out right.

You want to stretch the major muscle groups in your legs, torso, shoulders, arms, and neck, then work those muscles for a few seconds to allow their blood supply to improve. At the same time, you need to set up the ligaments and joints for what's coming by operating them a few cycles through their range of movements.

This isn't any big deal. By moving from head to toe, it can be completely done, once you've memorized the routine, in three to five minutes.

THE WARM-UP IS ONLY HALF THE GAME

Another act of which most of us are guilty is leaving the court after a match without taking a few minutes to gain the advantage of using our now-warm bodies to increase flexibility.

During hard exercise in which specific muscles are used, the lesser used groups tend to stiffen up. The ones you've depended on the most will tighten after you've cooled down. All players have had the experience of finishing a game, then taking a seat at a table to talk for a while and drink a glass of refreshment. When getting up, there is a momentary period of stiffness. Joints pop, muscles are sore, and there is a general feeling of being ninety years old.

A large part is caused by not taking the time for stretching while all your muscle groups are still hot from the exercise. Naturally, you'll never completely cure this little syndrome, but a proper warm-down will produce highly beneficial effects.

One of the key benefits from a warm-down is to get the lesser used muscles restretched so they don't fight against the ones you rely on and reduce their ability to move and respond.

The muscles in the body are somewhat like the Chinese symbols yin and yang. For every set needed to make a movement, there is a corresponding group, acting in the opposite direction to allow the return to our starting position. Heavy use of one set and light use of another can and does cause imbalances which will, over time, limit flexibility and render you more accident prone.

Stretching and flexing muscles when your body is warm from exercise is also beneficial to your game because it is during this period you should be able, through carefully controlled movements, to increase your overall flexibility. It's a perfect time to bend another tenth of an inch deeper or hold a stretch a second longer. You're already warmed so the chances of popping something are reduced.

The recommended routine, then, should be done twice every time you play: once, very gently, before you step onto the court, and a second time with more vigor immediately after playing before you have a chance to cool off.

TEN WARM-UP, WARM-DOWN MOVEMENTS

Some parts of this routine are similar to exercises in the fitness chapter. The way they are done here differs in that you are supposed to speed your way through these instead of doing them with slow deliberate concentration coupled to your breath control. Naturally, if you want to take the extra time, maintaining your breathing pace will enhance each movement of the routine, and slowing the motions down will result in a stronger workout.

The ten segments of this program all flow together in a natural fashion. After you start, you'll be able to move smoothly into each step.

Remember, the warm-up should take less than five minutes after you've learned the sequence. A tip here might be helpful. Take a three-by-five card, sit down, and make notes concerning this warm-up routine: The order of the exercises, the way something is done, etc. Then tape it on the inside of your racket cover so you'll have it with you to refer to when you need it.

Also keep in mind the difference between the warm-up and the warm-down. For the warm-up, do the movements gently. For the warm-down, increase the vigor.

Exercise 1: Arm Rotation

Stand facing forward, feet about twenty inches apart. Hands at sides. Now, with the right arm first, slowly bring it up in front of you, moving in a circle around the shoulder joint. Keep your arm stiff and continue the motion over your head and on behind you, like a backstroke in swimming. You'll end up with your hand back at your side where you started. Don't stop. Do it again, this time consciously stretching a little more. Next a third rotation, stretching still more. Not too hard, though, especially warming up. Three times is enough. Switch over and do it with your left arm.

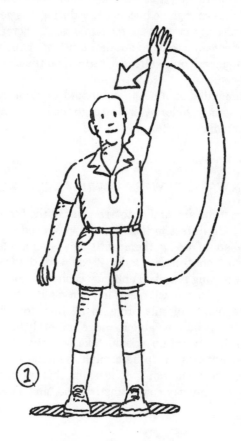

Exercise 2: Arm Extension

You've got the rotary motion of the shoulders, so you need the one used the most in tennis, the backward and forward motion. You should have ended up the first movement facing front with your arms at your sides. Bend your elbows and place your closed fists onto your shoulders. Now lift your elbows out from your sides until the undersides of your upper arms are parallel with the ground. Turn your toes in, still keeping your feet apart. Arch your back a little, then try to move your elbows backward. It's right if you feel your shoulder blades trying to touch one another. Back once, hold it, move your elbows forward again, then back harder but not too hard, hold it, then forward and back again. The third time, try and stretch a little—but gently, even in the warm-down. You'll be able to tell when you're close to overdoing it.

Exercise 3: Torso Twist

When you complete the third arm extension, you're in the perfect stance for twisting the upper body. So do it. Without moving your feet or legs, hands still on your shoulders, twist your torso, leading with your head as far left as is comfortable. Then come back unwinding, through the straight-ahead position, without stopping, as far right as you can manage. Then go back left again. This should be done in a definite swinging motion, with no stops anywhere. Three times to the left, three to the right is fine.

Exercise 4: Neck Twist

Many pulled back muscles come from attempts to protect the neck from being twisted or taking shock. Drop your arms to your sides, still stay in the pigeon-toed stance, look straight ahead, then twist your head to the left as far as is comfortable, back to straight ahead, then to the right. Move deliberately, but not too fast. After three lefts and rights, let your head slump forward until your chin is on your chest, then backward until you are staring at the ceiling or the sky. Bring your head back to center, eyes forward, and you'll be all set for the next step.

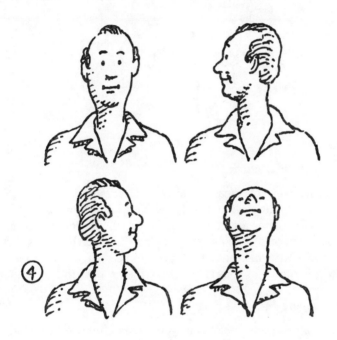

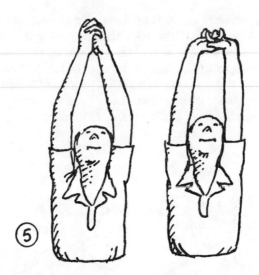

Exercise 5: Overhead Stretch

Raise both arms over your head, clasp your fingers together, and when you come to the top of your stretch, slowly, without unlacing your fingers, rotate your wrists so your palms are pointing up. This will pull your forearm muscles and add a half inch or so to your upward stretch. Hold the position for a few seconds, lower your arms, untwining your fingers as you do to allow your hands to hang naturally at your sides again, then repeat the movement.

Exercise 6: Jumping Jacks

You are still standing erect, hands at your sides after the overhead stretch. It's a fine position for starting nine jumping jacks. These are also known by the military name of side-straddle hops, but jumping jacks is somehow more descriptive. Bring your feet together. Now spring up into the air a few inches, using the toe and calf muscles. As you do, spread your legs apart, so when you land your feet will be twelve to fifteen inches apart. At the same time you open your legs, swing your arms up until you clap your palms together over your head. Keep your arms as straight as you are able without straining. Once you've clapped hands, and you've landed feet apart, spring up again. This time, while you're in the air, bring your feet together and swing your arms out and down so they end up next to your sides. Nine overhead claps of your hands is a set. Stop. Whew.

Exercise 7: Arm-free Swing

Number seven is next, so you're more than half through. You should also finish standing straight, legs together, facing forward with your hands at your sides. Raise your arms over your head. Higher. But easy. Stretch again. Then swing your arms down, across your body, crossing your arms. Without stopping the easy swing motion, move them back up to where you started from, over your head, then, as they lose force at the top of the circle, bring them down again. On the first swing, you had to cross either the right arm over the left or vice versa. This time when they come down, cross the other over in front. One more swing, for two, then a final one for three. Enough of that. You should have felt your shoulders roll forward as your arms crossed on each of the full, easy movements. Two more to go.

Exercise 8: Back Stretcher

You finish up in the normal position, facing forward, hands at your sides. Spread your feet apart about twenty to thirty inches. Raise both arms over your head. Bend down, and touch both hands to your left foot, then get down as close to the ground in front of you as you can, then try for the right foot. Now swing up in a circle to the left, not too fast, bending backward with your head and upper body as your arms make the huge rotation, then down again to your left foot. Three times to the left. After the third time of touching the right foot at the end of the sequence, instead of making the circle to the left, make it to the right, so the first toe you touch is your right one. Next to the middle, trying for the ground, then to the left. This time the rotary movement will end you up moving right to left, the opposite of the previous set of three. Don't bounce or press too hard. Three more, and you're standing, facing forward, hands at your sides again. Two more and you're ready to go and get 'em.

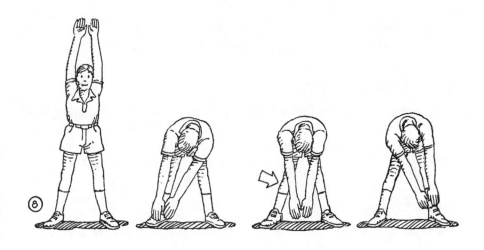

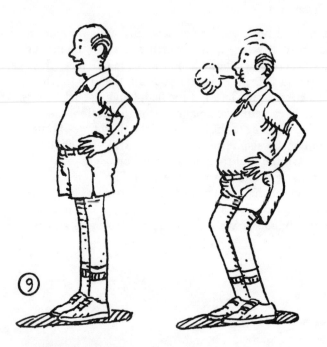

Exercise 9: Quarter Knee Flexes

Place your hands on your hips and do five quarter knee bends, lowering your weight down about ten to twelve inches and coming back to a standing position. Do them quickly, letting out your breath each time you move downward, and inhaling as you come back up. Keep your back straight and erect.

Exercise 10: Arm Isometrics

Press your hands and fingers together, palm to palm, at shoulder level, arms straight out in front of you. Press them very hard together, move them up, arms stiff, until your upper arms touch the two sides of your forehead, then back down until your hands touch your upper legs. Press hard—as hard as you can throughout the movement. When you touch your upper legs, relax and let your hands move to their regular position next to your sides. Then bring them up again, both arms out straight, hands at eye level. Cross your right hand under your left, so the backs of your hands are touching. The edges of your palms should be toward the ground. Concentrate. Try to press each of your fingers and thumbs against their opposite numbers. Then put on the pressure from your shoulders. It's kind of like making a backhand shot, but your two hands are providing the resistance. Move your arms up slowly, maintaining the force, until your upper arms touch your forehead. Then down again, as far as your body will allow your crossed arms to go toward bringing your hands to your upper legs. Relax. You've earned it. Repeat the two palm presses once more, and you're done.

Sounds like a lot, but after you understand how each movement leads into the rest, it won't be. What it will do is keep you from having a number of injuries and allow you to start every game ready to play—and score—which places you in a better position than many of the opponents you'll ever face.

8
How Green Was My Volley: The Importance of the Right Pro

STUDENT: *That was a nice shot. Who taught you?*
RUSSELL: *Oh, if you just hang around the game for thirty-five years, you'll get some bits to go right.*

It was a wet, rainy Thursday afternoon. The day had been cold and the forecast for Friday and the weekend promised a freeze. Russell, sitting in the University Club snack bar in Houston, had no trouble driving over from Austin in his Porsche, but as he was planning to go back the same evening, the thought of rain turning into sleet left him in a somewhat dour mood.

He watched the action on several of the indoor courts and talked quietly with Jason. Their more pressing business done, the conversation turned to the book they were writing.

Jason leaned back, speaking without looking at his friend and partner, eyes following the progress of two overweight players on the adjoining court. "We need a good anecdote about teaching professionals. One that shows the difference between good pros and bad ones." Shaking his head slightly at the missed opportunity he'd just witnessed, he glanced at Russell, who was nodding.

"Right. That should be easy. We've known a large group of both kinds." His attention was fully on the subject and the radiated alertness focused Jason's mind on the conversation. "What about that fellow, what's-his-name, who had the bloody awful backhand?"

Jason was still laconic, but interested. "He had a lousy forehand, too."

"For that matter, his overhead wasn't so keen either. All around, he didn't play very well."

Jason's eyes sparkled as he smiled. "But he was a teaching fool."

"If you mean it would take a fool to be taught by him, then you've got it."

"Oh, come on, Russell. A person might make a mistake and go to him once. But if he went back again, I agree with you."

"He did every damn thing quite wrong. Instead of realizing his shots were unorthodox and using that bit of information to allow him to give his students the freedom to develop their own styles, he was ashamed of not playing classically. So to make up for it, he insisted on every player he dealt with doing it by the book."

"He messed up a lot of people."

"One poor woman had to spend another five hundred undoing the damage created by the first five."

"One thing you can say about him, though. He's enthusiastic." Russell stretched slowly, reaching his arms high. As he relaxed, he shook his head. Trouble with using that example is its total lack of humor."

"It doesn't have to be funny."

"But it oughtn't be tragic either."

Jason nodded in agreement. "You're right. And what that guy does is tragic. If it weren't for his bullshit, he wouldn't be in business."

"He has something else, too." Russell's eyes were hard.

"What's that?"

"He has a wealth of people to draw from who have no idea in this world how to select a good pro, recognize one, or know what they should get from a lesson. Somebody's got to tell the bloody players how to judge."

Jason's smile broadened, in contrast to the other's intenseness. "That's just what we're trying to do."

NOT EVERY PRO IS RIGHT FOR YOU

The advice and knowledge of a teaching professional can help you when you attempt to realign your game to take advantage of your best over-forty skills. But not every professional is right for every player. Styles of teaching differ, senses of humor differ, and personalities differ. The single most important thing is to find a pro you feel comfortable around. There must be a rapport or the student-teacher relationship will never produce the basic elements of trust necessary to make the lessons effective.

A good pro is a mixture of many things: coach, trainer, instructor, opponent, doubles partner, philosopher; all these and more. In addition to helping you relearn the basics and hone your skills, the professional should know you well enough to bring you along at a pace which will enhance your enthusiasm for the game. The relationship should lead you into matches at a level designed to both challenge and satisfy your improving abilities.

Naturally, no professional can do this without your help. Pros are not mind readers. They have to know your feelings as you progress, so complete communications between player and teacher are vital. This takes us back to the need for rapport, which means more than merely "getting along." A great many people are charmed by the image of the smiling, handsome, friendly, suntanned tennis professional. And a lot of pros are charming. After all, they make their living dealing with the public, so a certain friendliness and personality projection is an absolute necessity. It isn't being phony to be nice to the members of the club, for instance. And it's more than just good business.

DIFFERENT REASONS FOR LESSONS

Not everyone takes tennis lessons simply to improve. Every player does not want to be a Forest Hills champ. He may see his time with the pro as recreational. If he can get in a good shot or two, it's something to talk about at the evening's cocktail party.

One of a pro's prime responsibilities is to foster a feeling of camaraderie among players to enhance the fun in the game for everyone.

For those who do wish to improve their game, however, and are serious about wanting to play better, the relationship necessary for a successful teaching experience goes beyond this level of contact. There has to be a true feeling of give and take between the two, as they become partners with a common goal. Discover this and your progress is ensured.

HOW TO SELECT THE RIGHT PRO

How do you find it? There is no easy way, but there are a few general guidelines.

A good place to start is to ask around among players you know.

Chances are one or two professionals have a reputation of working with over-forty enthusiasts. The professional at your club or courts may be a good source of information. And he or she may be the very person you need in the first place.

Once you've got a few names, go talk to them. Be honest and straightforward. Tell them you want an evaluation of your game in the light of your age and are interested in improving—but not necessarily determined to change your swing or anything else. You want advice and help. This initial conversation is very important. You should be able to communicate freely and feel comfortable.

The same holds true for a newcomer who is out seeking basic beginning instruction. You probably won't be able to talk about the many points of the game, and some of the jargon used may sound strange to you, but don't be discouraged.

Don't settle on feelings in this first meeting. It's a preliminary step. Unless you get into an argument with the pro and feel there is no possible way you can ever get along, make an appointment for at least a couple of lessons. You have to experience the teaching professional in action before you can decide if that style and yours will match.

All seasoned pros are well-rounded coaches. They have to be or they wouldn't make a living in the business. Each, however, will have stronger facets of instruction, areas where they excel. In one case it might be technique. In another, tactics. A third might be an ace in the art of ball placement. It stands to reason they will be more adept in teaching this aspect of the game than some of the others. Recognize this going in, not to be leery of it, but to understand and accept it. And to be certain the pro's orientation to the sport agrees with yours. There is no way to build the necessary mental compatibility if your attitudes are diametrically opposed.

Enjoy your initial lessons. Try to relax, learn, and have a good time. Even if you decide another pro might be better for you, there is no reason you can't have a pleasant experience and benefit. Every working pro can teach you more about the game. The more you know, the better you'll play.

MAKE UP YOUR OWN MIND

After a few sessions, form your own feelings about the suitability of a specific pro for you. Don't rely on another's opinion any more than you would about a person you were in love with and were going to marry. What is an excellent instructional style for one individual may be disastrous for you. And you are the one who counts in this instance.

If you decide you like the coaching you are receiving and want to stay with it, fine. You'll be on your way to better tennis. If there is something wrong and you're still not sure, try to pin it down. If it's a matter of personality, there's not a lot you can do.

It may be necessary for you to look around for a person who will be more compatible. If it's anything else, you owe it to both yourself and the pro to talk it out and try to resolve it. The pace of the lesson might be wrong. You want things to move a little slower or faster. Or possibly not every point is made clear to you so you need more examples and demonstration. Bring this up and discuss it as specifically as possible.

COMMUNICATE WITH THE PRO

One of the pluses of being forty or older is that you've had experience in expressing yourself and negotiating with others. Use these communications skills. Tell the pro how to teach you in a more meaningful fashion. Younger players tend not to do this. They seem to feel they are at fault if they don't get the lesson exactly right. Older people are more realistic. They know about two-way streets and gray areas between right and wrong.

No pro worthy of the name will be anything but attentive when you openly discuss the problem of how you can get more from a teaching session. The professional wants you to learn and improve. A large part of the satisfaction inherent in the job comes from watching beginning players get good and good players become better. Any input you can supply to enhance this procedure will be met with enthusiasm.

After you've made yourself clear about your special needs, try a few more lessons. Be attentive during the sessions. When you don't understand something, say so. As mentioned earlier, the older player is not as likely to be trying to impress someone as the younger enthusiast. It is meaningful in this situation. Your teacher will be both happy and impressed, however, when you show improvement by beating an opponent who regularly has defeated you.

YOU ARE THE BEST JUDGE OF YOUR PROGRESS

After this next cycle of teaching you have to do another reevaluation. By this point you and your instructor should be a compatible team. If not, there is something wrong.

You have to be careful here but you should be able to terminate the relationship without hard feelings. Again, the professional is a reasonable person. He knows he will not be able to teach each player with the same degree of success, but it is a defeat to fail to inspire and improve a willing student. There's bound to be a disappointment which might be expressed in a number of ways.

Why break off your relationship formally? Why not just go home from the courts one morning and never return? No real reason. It's done all the time. But it's nicer to tell the pro you've engaged you're grateful for all his time and effort and you've decided to play for a while to let the lessons sink in.

That's exactly what you ought to do. Play for a few weeks using what you've learned and trying your best to make it work. If it does, you might rethink your relationship, have another talk, and go back for more. If not, you at least have given the experience a good chance and can move forward secure in the knowledge you know how to do your part.

DIFFERENT PROS HAVE DIFFERENT TEACHING STYLES

Tennis pros can be divided into two large groups. First there are those who primarily see the game as one of technique. Then, there are the others, who appreciate good technique but view the sport from a broader perspective, usually acquired through years of evaluation. The professional who sees grip, stance, and so on, and nothing else, will tend to coach by changing grip and stance and so on. Fortunately, there aren't many of these in the professional ranks today. In years past, there have been. A good pro is an observer of technique, of course. But he or she realizes there is more to the game.

A pro also faces some impossible situations. Take the case of the forty-five-year-old ex-power hitter, for instance, who notices when the oomph is put in the swing it results in a wild ball. Contrarily, when he hits easily, he has accuracy. He can't seem to find a happy medium. So he seeks out the help of a professional.

If he goes looking for a mystical cure for his degeneration, the relationship is doomed. A pro is not a patent medicine. You can't take two lessons and regain lost youth.

If the player comes in with a specific problem, such as, "My backhand has gone to hell," or "I can't punch the ball like I used to," a good pro can help.

First, by observation. You hit a few balls back and forth so he can watch. If the problem lies in a basic technique, it will show itself quickly. If it's something else, it will take a little time.

A GOOD PRO LOOKS, THEN LECTURES

Careful observation is the starting point for expert analysis. Then comes concerted retraining. Little things can mean a lot to the older player. Something as simple as relearning where to stand and how to move on the court can produce improvement. On a serve, for instance, placing yourself a step or two farther back than normal and moving forward as the ball is hit gives you a physical edge, because it's easier to go right or left after you have overcome inertia and have your body in motion than it is to jump one way or another from a static position. Or on a move across from rest, every player can pick up a split second by pushing off with whichever foot is on the side of the body away from the ball. It's amazing how many good players lean toward the ball, move the foot on that side of their body, then start their run.

These are minor things and are merely adjustments to already present skills. Sometimes, however, more extensive alteration is needed.

If someone has a shot he can almost never execute successfully, or if there's something he is not doing well in his present style of play, then it's time for technique retraining.

Consider the player who uses the western-style grip. It may have been fine in younger years, but suddenly, when the volley becomes an important part of his game, he finds he cannot volley successfully. A grip, then, stops him from playing a whole-court game. This defines the time for a new technique.

CHANGE ONLY WHAT'S NECESSARY

Change for the mere sake of change, even if it's done to make you feel you've learned something, is foolish. With every alteration there comes a finite duration in which your game will be poorer, not better. During a change, you concentrate on making the corrections. You are constantly analyzing and comparing. This takes concentration away from the match. Worse, any new methods require retraining of the muscles until your memory allows you to perform the act with fluid, unthinking motion. In other words, if you change something you must expect your game to come down a bit while you learn your way into the new style.

The rule for making a major alteration is simple and inviolate. You should change only when there is something big to gain from the changing. Pros know this, so the wise ones don't push changes without concentration and study.

When an alteration is considered the best solution, there is still a constraint recognized by all good coaches. The change must be in keeping with a player's basic style and ability. An individual who, from his strokes and motions on the court, looks like he is better suited to chopping the ball should be developed in that direction. To attempt to train him into a smoother style by insisting that he master the finesse of a top-spin drive is counterproductive. By the time people pass forty, they are going to have much of their lifestyle set. This same fact holds true in tennis. You can take established characteristics and work within that framework to make improvements, but it's almost impossible, and unsatisfactory from the pupil's standpoint, simply to ignore all predispositions and go off on a new tangent. So even sweeping changes must be custom-fitted to the individual and not taken from a book and applied with a "this-is-the-right-way" attitude.

TEACHING A TRANSITION IS HARD

Instructing a pupil in transition is probably one of the most difficult challenges facing a professional. Here the coach must become an artist. In addition to patient demonstration, repeating movements over and over again so the student can build a mental image of making the shot, the teacher must be able to paint a word picture vivid enough to be seen. This communication tells students how they presently appear during these movements and how they should appear as their muscles learn the motions and store them into memory.

Knowing how you should look, and feeling it if you don't, is half the training. Once you've gained this plateau, you can rely on your mental image and concentration to guide your further progress.

It's also hard for the professional to gauge an individual's capacities accurately. How much can be covered in a lesson? How good can a specific player become? When is a novice ready to face more serious opposition? When will the changes be sufficiently absorbed and practiced so the pupil can be brought along by further instruction? How far can this student go? These are all questions facing professionals when they accept the task of working with a student.

HONESTY BETWEEN YOU AND THE PRO IS VITAL

Sometimes honesty is difficult to come by. A tennis pro needs it. A man tells his pro he is taking lessons so he can win his club's championship. The professional, after watching the player, and based on having competed against other members of the same club who were strong athletes, has a choice. A glib response coupled to a line of bright patter might hold the student for a number of lessons. Make no mistake, payment for lessons is a big source of a teaching pro's income. If it's obvious to the professional the student will never be able to reach his goals, he has to gently burst the grandiose balloon. It's not an easy or pleasant job. But it would be dishonest to con the student into a series of lessons, take his money, and all the while realize the eventual outcome of the training would be a moment of massive disappointment.

It's easier to be honest with an older player. Perhaps one of the illusions of youth is a certainty everything is possible. By the time we reach forty we understand the differences between possibilities and probabilities—and the desirability of concentrating on the probable.

A twenty-year-old, responding to a professional opinion which holds her style of play or her ability is not sufficient to allow her to become a touring player, can be anticipated to have a response based on an emotional reaction. Storming off in a cloud of disappointment, she will seek the counsel of other, more sympathetic and encouraging teachers. She should. Any one professional's understanding of an individual's capacities is a judgment call. There may be more to the player than is readily apparent—a hidden drive, for instance, which has not yet had time to mature.

While it might be equally hard to tell a forty-year-old ex-collegiate champion he probably cannot win a given tournament because he is physically out of shape and overweight, he is probably going to respond in a less emotional fashion with more introspective analysis. It's still a distasteful and unpleasant job, but it goes with the territory. The professional must be able to appraise a student's limits with accuracy and then be candid in expressing an opinion. At best, it's hard. But at least with a person over forty who has some experience in life, the response is not likely to become an emotional tirade.

Students must understand and appreciate this need for honesty. Told something they don't want to hear, they should think it over. If they feel their ability is greater, they should make the professional aware of their estimate so he can reevaluate the situation.

Nothing is ever hurt by a second careful look. If the coach's feelings are unchanged after a second appraisal, the student must either seek another opinion or alter his aspirations. It's a hard moment for both parties.

The professional owes you straight talk. There is no other way to direct you toward attainable goals. Even though people get so involved in tennis it becomes a major part of their lives, it's still a game. The reason you play it is to have fun. It's more fun to meet your goals than to lose and always fall short of a desired performance. The pro's concern has to be your enjoyment of the game. The good professional realizes you'll enjoy it more if you approach it with a realistic understanding of your personal ability.

Take all the above and you can see why your interaction with a professional must be compatible. It's hard to overemphasize the importance of a good relationship.

A GREAT PRO CAN ALMOST READ YOUR MIND

Some professionals, and these are ones who are truly blessed, have an inherent ability to go beyond how a student appears to be playing and enter his mind. They can feel and sense what the person with whom they are communicating feels and senses. From this vantage point they are able to make contributions to stroke improvement and game planning. How is this possible? No one knows. But there is no doubt it happens. Any number of excellent pros can tell you of the feeling. It occurs when the personal relationships are right and the combination of teacher-pupil becomes more than either of the participants. If you're lucky, it will happen to you. When it does, cherish the moment, because you will find yourself on the receiving end of a great learning experience.

DEMONSTRATION, REPETITION, AND GUIDED PRACTICE ARE THE BEST WAYS TO TEACH

The best way to teach tennis is through a combination of demonstration, to illustrate what's right and wrong, repetition, and patient practice on the part of the student. Team a professional who demonstrates well with a pupil of any age who will concentrate on his practice, and you have a good learning situation regardless of whether or not they ever actually get into one another's minds.

Demonstration has a built-in problem. The student should not try to look like the coach. The effect of the action of slowly moving through a stroke should be to show how it's done, not become an exact pattern to follow. Each student has to bring his own body into the effort to make the shot his, not a copy of the coach's.

GOOD PROS MAY CONTRADICT THEMSELVES

Good professionals will, from time to time, contradict themselves. A fine example can be seen from this illustration. A forty-five-year-old woman was having trouble with her backhand. After a series of losing matches where her shots were going wild, she came in to see what might be done about it.

She had three separate problems. First, she was trying too hard. She was putting too much muscle behind the swing to get velocity on the ball. Second, she held the racket too close to her body. She wasn't giving herself enough room to stroke. And finally, she had lost confidence in her ability to make a good backhand return.

Correcting the three difficulties took several lessons. In one, she was told not to try so hard, to relax. In the next, after the tension had been drained away and she felt more secure, she was instructed to use less conscious force, to stroke more lightly. Next came the relationship of the racket to her body. Then the contradictions started. She was told to swing harder, and to use more force on the ball to build up stroke velocity.

Other contradictions are also possible. If a working professional sees what you are being told cannot be translated into action, he or she will try a different approach. This may mean negating what was previously said in an earlier lesson.

Don't be disturbed by corrective teaching. It doesn't represent a mistake on your part or the pro's, but rather a sincere attempt to bring you up to a certain level and get the maximum from your personal characteristics.

If you come across a contradiction, mention it. Find out why, so you don't continue thinking your teacher is inconsistent.

SIMPLE THINGS MEAN A LOT

Some of the best things a pro can do for you are the simplest. Minor alterations can sometimes produce major improvements. As slight a thing as changing your cross-court motion so you approach the ball on an angle as opposed to moving straight across its path can give you a split second quicker return and your opponent less time to get set. Don't be afraid of these changes. Try and learn them because they often fine-tune your game and spell the difference between winning and losing.

PACING AND BEING READY TO PLAY

Most pros are expert in pacing. When playing a match, they know you will be tired toward the end. Unless you are in excellent physical condition, the more tired you become, the more prone you will be to injury. Most strains and sprains occur in the early moments of play or the closing minutes of the game. The first is due to a lack of adequate warm-up exercise, the latter from extending too far due to the heat of battle.

Both can be handled by improvements in physical conditioning. But neither can be totally avoided.

Adequate warming up, including stretching and getting the heart rate to increase, is a must for all over-forty players. It's a must for any serious individual, but it is more important to the older person because the more years on your body, the longer it takes to heal from an injury. An ankle twist which would have put you out for a couple of days when you were twenty will put you in bed for a week at sixty.

Understanding how to pace yourself through the full game to keep a good margin of stamina at the end is vital. Many games are won or lost in the final minutes, so you have to have enough strength to carry through to the finish in your best style. A pro can show you some valuable tricks, like taking your time during the early points. Stretch a little between getting the ball in your hand and serving. Be aware of the debilitating effects of heat and humidity. If you're faced with a serious combination of these two stress makers, drink water throughout the game.

Professionals oriented to working with older, over-forty players know the imporance of warm-up, warm-down, and pacing. They have access to programs containing information on suitable exercises and diet. Generally, you'll have to ask for this material because it isn't a regular part of the teaching program. But three to five minutes spent stretching before hitting the first ball can prevent injury.

Professionals, even though they may have a good knowledge of the basic causes of strains and pulls, are not doctors. Sometimes, because of the demand of their clients, they may discuss why certain game-related strains occur, but they are not equipped to prescribe treatment. Ills such as tennis elbow or toe blisters need to be treated by a physician. The professional can, however, spot tendencies in style or play which will, without alteration, result in long-term physical damage. They should and do address themselves to this problem.

THE RIGHT STYLE IS SAFER

The correct style for you as a player is also, in almost every case, the safest way for you to play. What feels natural is usually suitable to an individual's skeletal and muscle structure. So by helping you overcome an observable tendency which will result in physical dysfunctions, the pro will also improve your game.

Torque, or the twisting of the racket, for instance, is a common cause of tennis elbow. At the point of impact the hand is gripping the handle firmly. Any rotational movement is transferred up the arm to the elbow, a joint designed for movement in a single plane. The twisting force stresses various components of the joint, so pain occurs.

The reason the racket twists in the first place is simple. Instead of consistently hitting the ball with the center focus of the strings, the player is making contact with the right or left outer edge of the face, which causes rotation and torques the elbow. It also results in poor accuracy, loss of power, and a drop in the speed of the ball. The professional, by correcting this tendency to hit off center, not only alleviates the cause of considerable pain but also improves the player's ability.

PROS NEED TO EXPERIMENT

Professionals must be avid experimenters. Since they have the ability to play well trained into their muscle systems, they are able to try new or different techniques without damaging their skill. From these experiences they may develop improvements which can be passed along to their students.

A commonly observed footwork problem, for example, is the tendency to strike the ball while falling back or moving in the direction of the ball's travel. This kills the force of the shot and results in weak returns which barely make it over the net. A professional can experiment with you and demonstrate how much more hitting power there is in having your weight move against the path of the ball and into your stroke. If you have trouble correcting this fault, the pro can go further and design a custom alteration of your style to prevent it.

Hitting across the flight of the ball on backhand shots is another normal tendency. By experimentation, a professional may learn to prevent this by having you move both arms in unison when the shot is made. The simultaneous two-arm swing requires good body placement in order to maintain balance and forces less upper body rotation during the time of racket-to-ball contact. It looks odd, is unorthodox, but might be the solution to an otherwise incurable difficulty. The pro who is willing to experiment can often discover unique solutions to seemingly unsolvable playing tendencies.

A PLAYER'S FEET TELL A STORY

One mark of a good teacher is the ability to concentrate on the feet and eyes of a player who is hitting and moving on the court. This habit, improved through years of practice, even extends into watching the pros play in big-money tournaments. Conversation between professionals after a match can be hard to comprehend. There is little discussion of the spectacular shots but much talk about footwork and concentration.

As long as gravity is an effective force in the universe and humans insist on teeter-totter balancing on their two hind feet to be able to use their hands, the placement of those feet onto the ground is a skill of basic importance. In all sports, the ability to step smoothly and move quickly depends upon sureness of foot. This is doubly true for tennis.

The professional, by watching a player's feet, can detect and cure numerous faults.

Stepping into a serve, for example, is a common trick. Even though the movement gives the body a forward velocity, the step does not add speed or power to the stroke. But, because the body is somewhat off balance, it can adversely affect accuracy.

If it's natural for you to step forward at the point of or just after impact, then fine—if your serves go where you aim them. The step does have the positive effect of moving a player a little closer to the net. But it's obviously foolish to sacrifice good ball placement for the small time advantage if the movement cannot be made easily.

A pro, by concentrating on the feet, will see this tendency. Even though it's a variable a great many players don't need to add to their service stroke, it is a natural act for others and their accuracy suffers without it. But detecting the presence of the step is only possible if the pro watches the footwork of his student.

Service return is another area where close analysis of foot placement can pay big dividends.

A number of good players wait for a serve to come to them by standing in an alert, knees-bent, set-for-action position. To a casual observer, they look tensed and ready. The observant professional sees past this stance by watching the first step the player takes. It shows where the individual carried the weight of his body while awaiting the ball. If he were supporting himself by forcing his center of gravity, and therefore his weight, over the heels, he inadvertently placed himself in a position from which he is unable to move with a rapid fluidity. It takes a finite time to roll the weight forward onto the toes, then take a step. No forward motion can be produced until the weight is transferred onto the ball of the foot. Getting "caught flat-footed" is more than an old expression for helpless surprise. It's a problem many players have and only observant professionals can detect.

A second footwork-related checkpoint the experienced pro watches is covered by another old saying: "as smooth as silk." It means when on the court your moves should be as fluid as you can make them.

There are people who play like mechanical clockwork robots. A tin-soldier effect is easy to observe, but quite hard to cure. Relief from jerkiness usually can be gained only if the pro can discover the point of origin of the broken movement.

The reason this style of play needs to be smoothed out is because it is more time-consuming to make five or ten separate motions than one free-flowing stream of movement. In the senior game, time helps replace strength.

Quiet observation may reveal a player is moving the racket back, half cocking his arm for a swing before rotating his shoulders in the direction of the ball. Others may be starting their feet before the weight transfer which comes from the shoulder movement. These are both off-balancing maneuvers. Weight is shifted in one direction, then redirected in another, resulting in a very slow start.

By picking out the initiating movement which sets off the jerky sequence, the pro can help a student induce smoothness. The pupil can relearn from his initial movement on to the point of contact with the ball. In many cases, curing the first incidence of erratic motion will smooth out successive actions.

The ideal move is based on a free and easy style. Shoulders rotate in the direction you are about to run. Turning from the waist, your foot farthest away from where you want to be steps across, the body turns, the other foot comes into stride in tempo with your arm starting to fall back, the first foot makes its step, and you've got the racket at full cock as you plant your feet securely for a hit and follow through.

If any part goes wrong, the time required for action increases. People who run with their rackets full back from the initiation of their first step, for instance, give up tenths of a second—the same tenths that make the difference between getting to the ball and scoring a point or missing a winning shot.

It takes a trained eye to see the nuances of style and concentration to detect how it might be improved.

In sum, a good professional is observant, teaches through demonstration, is patient, willing to experiment, and will not induce change in your style just to make you a more classic player. He knows the value of naturalness, wants you to have a technique which fits your body, and loves to see you win. He will bring you along at a pace suitable to your learning skills, help you set attainable goals, and can, if the chemistry is right, even become one of your friends.

9
What to Look for When You Buy a Tennis Week

"As an over-forty player you must beware of the young pro who comes up saying, 'Wait a minute, we do it this way here,' then proceeds to break down your style trying to get you to do it his way."   Russell Seymour

"They treat 'em like Davis Cup prospects with drills where you run here and there."   Jason Morton

It was a little after noon when the club's white Ford station wagon returned from the airport. In addition to numerous garment bags and suitcases, the driver was conducting six ladies from Memphis, Tennessee, who had signed up for a full week of tennis.

The facilities, located in the heart of the Texas hill country overlooking a blue expanse of wide lake, sparkled in the bright noonday sun. Even in April there was a hint of the blistering heat which would wrap over the countryside in the summer months. But the day was perfect; a combination of high seventies and low humidity.

Amid the general confusion of bag sorting, roommate selection, and registration, the six women had little time to focus on the surroundings. The line of tennis courts off to the left side of the main building marching away up a small terraced hill beckoned. Everyone was enthusiastic and excited about the prospects of a full week of instruction and play.

It took the group about two hours to get themselves settled in and ready for their first event. After unpacking in the air-conditioned comfort of the two-bedroom bungalows, one by one they emerged from their rooms, rackets and balls in identical canvas satchels, dressed in what was to become known as their uniforms. Each wore matching tops and skirts with their names needleworked into the fabric of their blouses. Today's color was apparently brown and shades of tan, and the outfits were, aside from the names, exact duplicates of one another.

As a group they trooped down to the main teaching area. Referring to the lineup for the day's events, they were expecting a two-hour on-court introduction and preliminary evaluation by Russell Seymour and his staff.

The six women moved onto their assigned courts, smiling and talking among themselves. They were off on vacation, away from their jobs and the cares of their families, on their own to enjoy it.

They were standing, chatting to kill time as they'd arrived a little early, when one by one their eyes widened. Coming through the green wire gate entrance to the court was a man. He smiled, but kept to himself. Soon he was followed by another and another until there were eight. Three had other women with them.

The six ladies from Memphis were stunned. They had registered for what they thought was a "Ladies Only" program and were finding themselves in an obviously mixed group. Concern about their husbands' reactions when and if they found out their wives had gone off on a week's trip to an out-of-state place full of strange men was based on their southern conservative upbringing. They talked among themselves for a moment, undecided as to what they should do. At that moment, Russell Seymour came through the entryway. He was immediately identified by his dress as a member of the coaching staff. One of the now-excited Memphis group rushed over to him.

"You're Russell Seymour. I can recognize you from the brochure."

"Yes, ma'am, I am.

"And you're the head instructor here."

"Yes, ma'am." His voice was warm and his accent gave him a unique style.

"Well, we've got a problem."

"Ma'am?" Russell looked at her quizzically over the use of the word "we."

"Myself and my friends here." She indicated the remaining five ladies who were coming over.

"What's that, then, ma'am?"

"We thought we were registering for a week in an all-women's program. Now we see it's mixed."

Russell studied her with his blue eyes. "Yes, ma'am, this is a mixed week. There's nothing we can do about that. While you ladies have come all the way from. . . ," he paused.

"Memphis."

"... Memphis, it would seem a shame for you not to enjoy yourselves."

"Oh, we intend to."

Russell looked startled. "Then what's the problem?"

"It's our husbands. We're almost sure when we each get back home and they hear about how much fun we've had here, they'll want to bring us back during their vacations."

"And?" Russell was smiling, perplexed.

"And we'd appreciate it if, when we return, you and your staff will be very careful not to tell them we came to a mixed session with a bunch of other men. They'd never understand."

Seymour, smiling broadly, nodded his head. "I'll see to that right off, ma'am. Now suppose we get started with this lesson."

Relieved and chattering again, the ladies turned their attention to the court.

INVESTIGATE FIRST

The incident was funny, but it could have been sad. Not because their husbands might have found out they were attending a mixed class, but because six enthusiastic tennis players had signed up for a week of play and instruction without even enough knowledge or investigation to be sure they were in an all-female group.

The odd thing about all this is how common it is. People select an expensive, time consuming vacation on the strength of color pictures in a brochure. Most who do this aren't going to try and improve their athletic skills or learn more about their favorite game. They are going to relax, and almost any first-class hotel in an exciting location can provide for their needs quite well.

It's not the same for tennis weeks.

A good tennis week is more than just five or six days of instruction. For the average enthusiast, the opportunity to play tennis and receive expert coaching for a week is a real treat. Eating, sleeping, talking, and centering your attention on the game for five consecutive days will allow anyone to make grand progress. But the programs can be grander in some places than others.

How do you judge the session before you've tried it? There are some pointers.

ASK SOMEONE WHO HAS BEEN THERE

Any good facility will be happy to supply you with names of individuals from your area who have participated in their program. Of course, you'll be referred to people the management thinks had a good time. That's okay if you remember it when talking with them. Keeping it in mind when confronting someone who is borderline enthusiastic about the place or who tells you some kind of a horror story will make it clear how bad the situation must have been.

Another factor which bears on the personal recommendation is how much you know about the person giving testimony. If he is similar to you in taste and life-style, then fine. If he liked it, you might like it, too. If you and he differ in outlook, then his comments have to be adjusted by an understanding of what your differences are in the way you see the world. Aside from this, the personal recommendation is a fine way to get an inside peek at what goes on.

Tennis weeks are different from facility to facility and even, in some cases, from season to season in the same facility. Many promise more than they can deliver in the promotional pieces, so a careful review of what they say they can accomplish will allow a discriminating, realistic reader to cross off a number of overpromising offers quickly.

Others are set up on a program of daily hard work. Naturally, you want to work on your game or you wouldn't be going in the first place, but your idea of "work" and theirs can be vastly different. A schedule which starts with mandatory calisthenics and a mile run at seven, before breakfast, just may not be your idea of how to spend a profitable, entertaining six or seven days. This might sound extreme, but there are a number of tennis weeks run like an old-time Marine boot camp. And there are people who enjoy it year after year. It seems to suit them just fine, as their individual preferences run to strong regimen. Possibly they feel they are getting into shape and improving their life-style. If this doesn't fit your idea of fun, however, then don't go. Even by accident!

HOW MUCH INDIVIDUAL INSTRUCTION?

The best planned and conducted tennis weeks for people over forty tend to place more importance on the individual and less on the group. Being treated as an individual, with special focus on the strengths and problems in your game, seems to generate the fastest progress. Some can use the fast-foot-work, high-speed endurance drills and will find their games improving from the gain in physical and mental conditioning. Others will discover these routines too demanding. The result will be a drop in quality of playing skills because of tension and fatigue. Even though you are a member of a group, the facility which offers you maximum flexibility for individual action probably has the best learning environment, all other things being equal.

WHAT ABOUT THE STAFF?

One of the "other things" is the professional staff on hand. Famous names and seasoned pros are no guarantee of a good experience because of how they might be employed. If it's a situation in which the "big name" meets each person individually, talks to the group for an hour a morning, then disap-pears after sending you out to hit balls with some twenty-two-year-old "assistant pro," it's not so satisfactory. If, and this also happens, the Big Name takes an active part in the daily teaching routine, is present during almost every practice session to answer questions, and drops around during your free play or practice time to give you his comments, you'll be able to learn quite a lot.

HOW MANY PEOPLE WILL YOU BE WORKING WITH?

Another thing to look for is the situation in which you and two or three other people are assigned a pro to work with you on as close to a one-on-one basis as possible.

This is the other extreme of the system in which you, along with twenty-five other pupils, toe the mark together, performing group exercise to the guidance of a professional. Individual instruction, aimed at your personal habits and abilities, will always beat group therapy when it comes to your making progress. Yet there are tennis weeks run on both principles.

In the ideal program, you would be paired off with no more than four, and preferably three, people. Each of the others would be at about your same level of proficiency. Your instructor would be at least thirty-five with twenty or so years in the game, of which the last fifteen were spent teaching. Your rate of learning under these conditions, if the other factors are right, will astound you, not to mention your regular opponents back home who have grown accustomed to your game.

WILL IT BE A GOOD LIFE EXPERIENCE?

A good tennis week, however, doesn't start and end with only tennis. You are there for a vacation. That means good food, fine accommodations, time for socializing, and activities geared to your other leisure time interests. With this in mind, it's probably a good idea to investigate the facility. The "boot-camp" style of operation usually doesn't offer much aside from a bed to sleep off the exertions of the day and a brief happy hour. People who enjoy this regimen like the feeling they really had to "put out" to stay with the program.

But no one, no matter how enthusiastic, can live on tennis alone. People have to have other interests in life or they'll go stale. The tennis camp has you captive for a full week, so it behooves you to be sure of what they are offering as diversions away from the game itself. It's always nice to be able to relax with someone you have played against during the day. Strong, lasting friendships can be formed at the end of a special tournament or organized round of play, if there is an opportunity for the opponents to gather together and recall the moments of the just-completed games. You'll also be able to judge whom to avoid in the future by how the retelling of the past events comes out.

CALL FIRST

Questioning a school before enrolling is a must and a telephone call is an inexpensive investment. Your queries should be simple and basic. Their answers should be straightforward. If you get a glaring generality, then back off and try again. They owe you a direct response.

If you were to ask, for instance, "How many hours of instruction will I get?" and the comeback is, "It varies with each student, depending upon his needs," it would pay you to probe a little deeper. Here are some to-the-point questions which deserve precise answers. If you can't get them from the first person you talk to, try the chief instructor or the head of the facility. Don't enroll until you're satisfied you've been properly informed.

First, ask how many hours of instruction you will receive on a personal basis. Be sure you tell them you are not referring to being one of the chorus line, but are talking about individual teaching, even in a group as large as five people. Since there are forty working hours in a normal five-day week, this figure should represent at least two to three hours a day. Or, put another way, a minimum of ten to fifteen individual hours of personalized attention.

The next thing is to get a description of a typical morning or after-noon session. What you're probing for is the philosophy behind their training.

You want access to three or four pros who are old enough to understand the way the game changes for players over forty. What you don't need is some batch of young yoyos who spend their time hitting balls to you under the guise of practice. Or worse, a pack of overly enthusiastic pros still in their early twenties who have been brainwashed about there only being the "way we do it here." What they will succeed in doing is turning your game inside out. Or, if you are still in the formative period of establishing a method of play, they can manage to mess it up beyond recognition.

The next area to discuss is court time. After the teaching sessions, how much court time will you be given without any extra charge? At one of the most famous schools, the instruction is respectable, but the students have to stand in line up to an hour in order to get onto the courts for a match or practice. An adequate regimen is to offer three hours of instruction and then three free hours of court time. Naturally, you might have to register for the three hours of noncompulsory practice or playing, but there should be ample courts to offer you the minimum of three full hours without any long, protracted wait.

While you are at it, check the qualifications of the pro who heads the camp. Ideally, he or she should have at least ten years of teaching experience and ten years in tournament play. There are some good professionals who don't reach this level, but for the over-forty player, it is almost a bare minimum background.

The staff also should be more than one deep in people with similar levels of experience. A seasoned leader with a backup crew of newcomers means you'll spend most of your time with the less experienced teachers.

Obviously, economics is a force here. If the management decides to pay a top name the large sums of money such a player can demand and get, the addition of a complete staff of practiced teaching professionals may be too great an investment to allow the camp to offer its program at a competitive rate. This problem only concerns you if you become involved in the activities they offer. Fortunately, most recognized tennis personalities tend to be jealous of their reputations and are too cagey to fall into this trap. After all, as a customer and a fan, who are you going to end up blaming? The camp or the star? So they use their considerable influence to try and balance the staff. Sometimes, sadly, this doesn't take place.

WILL THERE BE A TOURNAMENT?

Another question should center on whether or not a tournament will be a part of the curriculum.

There are a number of over-forty players who have never entered tournament competition. Their skills are good enough to allow them to compete in their class, but the formality of the competition seems to affect their attitude and keep them away. This is a shame, as tournament play lends another dimension to the scope of the game. The organized nature of the event makes each game more crucial. A player gets an opportunity to share growing tension and a feeling of victory with others who are in the identical situation, thus bringing about strong camaraderie.

The ideal tennis week would offer at least one tournament experience to allow the student to participate on neutral ground. After sampling, even the most reluctant enthusiast will be converted and come back for more.

CLIMATE AND WEATHER

Inquiries about the climate, which go beyond, "Is the weather nice?" can reveal potential trouble spots. A camp in the hill country of central Texas or south of Tampa, Florida, will have about the same temperatures as Virginia during the late spring or early summer. The intensity of the sun, however, is much greater. Sunburn can happen in a matter of minutes of uncovered or unshaded exposure in Texas or Florida.

If there is going to have to be some special adaptation to the climate, it's better to know it in advance, so you can get to work on the trouble. In the hot months, it would be a good idea, no matter where the location, to accustom yourself to spending two or three hours in the sun. It can save some pain after the first day of instruction.

YOU HAVE TO EAT, TOO

Questions about the food are in order. Do they serve every meal from a buffet line? Can you order from a menu? What are some typical meals? Euphemisms abound in the dining room. A "sumptuously luxurious buffet" can all too easily turn out to be a cafeteria line. Not that there's anything wrong with a cafeteria but if you arrive expecting something a little less stylish than the main dining salon on *QE II*, only to find a knotty-pine-paneled room with steam tables and a chow line, you're going to be disappointed.

The formalities of dining should be discussed, as well as the service. Will a coat and tie be mandatory or is there a more casual air to the place? Would a long dress be appropriate for some evenings or will sports clothes be sufficient?

A wide range of style and accommodations are offered, so you'll be able to find a tennis week which offers you just what you want in the way of life-style and instruction. But not unless you take the time to ask.

STUDY THE SOCIAL SIDE CAREFULLY

Social activities are another area where personal preference is important. Some people like the country club atmosphere which includes evening dances and planned events. To others, it's an anathema.

Take the time to discuss the social activities and the attitude of the camp toward these aspects of their program. If the answers are vague, look out. There probably hasn't been much thought given to this necessary and important segment of the week.

Some of the above doesn't have to have much to do with tennis, but as noted earlier, neither man nor woman lives by tennis alone. It may be the reason a group of strangers gather together for a week of play and instruction, but when all that's over and they have run themselves ragged, there is still time left in the evening to fill. How this is handled can make a difference in the overall success of the week. It can affect your ability to learn and get the most out of what is being offered.

REPEATING ONE POINT CAN SAVE YOU A SAD EXPERIENCE

Next to checking out the facilities in person, the telephone interview can be the most effective technique for determining the pluses and minuses of the various programs. While no one can describe the accommodations you'll be given thoroughly enough to cover such fine points as walls so thin your next-door neighbors' snoring or nighttime activities come through as if there were no walls at all, they can tell you what to expect in bed size, clothes storage, and other points of habitability which might make a difference to you.

You can't learn anything if you don't ask, so while you've got the opportunity, ask everything you might want to know. If you forget something, call back. Don't feel as if you're imposing. You need good information if you are going to make a sound decision. The management of the facility should be glad to take all of the time any rational person needs to give information. After all, if you're calling long distance, it indicates an interest. The management has a like interest in your attending their week of activity. Expect some salesmanship. The degree of aggressiveness you find over the phone might just let you in on more about the operation than the actual answers to your inquiries.

ALONE OR IN A GROUP?

One of the questions facing an individual or a couple in selecting a tennis week is whether to go it alone or make it into a group affair. Six or eight twosomes from the same club might make a compatible group. The advantage lies chiefly in the sharing of a common experience and the availability of known friends in a strange social environment.

The disadvantages center on your individual preference. It might suit your needs better to be able to get off on your own. Having people from your home courts present could inhibit your ability to immerse yourself into the game, thus hurt your learning experience.

Only you can decide the right size of the group of friends who should be invited. In any case, there is one thing you don't have to concern yourself over. The organizers and professionals at any good tennis week facility will arrange the playing schedules to assure you of getting ample time to try your new skills out on a variety of players. In other words, even if you go with a large group, you'll still be matched against strangers. This practice not only helps your game but improves the time everyone has during the social hours.

PRO-PUPIL RATIO

Two final thoughts on tennis weeks. The first concerns a subject mentioned earlier: the ratio of pupils to professionals.

There is more to this subject than appears on first inspection.

Beginners need more teaching time than advanced players. With a more experienced enthusiast, the basic concepts and muscle memory are formed. When you offer someone of this level something new, it can be done in a sort of tennis shorthand. The attention can be to detail rather than the overview.

When teaching a new player the forehand, you have to show the grip, the swing, the step into the ball, and the rhythm of the stroke. With an experienced player, most of this is second nature. What is needed is fine tuning, not a complete overhaul. In the one case you are forced to look at a number of variables. You might correct the stance, the grip, the swing, and go back to the stance. In the second you might only have to work on how the wrist is breaking or the tightness with which the racket is held.

The class for a beginner needs to be smaller than the teaching unit for the more advanced player.

Beginners need to be in groups of three to four players to each teaching professional. The better, more experienced players can get along well in groups with as many as six to eight per instructor.

Both the above figures are dependent upon the teacher's ability to instruct. A ratio of four to one is no good at all if the pro is only a human ball-return machine.

Given the choice between larger class groups and poor teachers, always move toward the larger groups. A good professional instructor can do something for every student in any size group. A poor teacher can't do anything for anybody, even in the one-on-one situations.

ARRIVE IN GOOD SHAPE ALREADY

The last thing that needs saying about tennis weeks, especially when it comes to over-forty players, has to do with physical fitness.

To get the most possible benefit from the experience, go in good shape. You may think you're ready, willing, and able because you play ten or twelve times a month, but chances are, unless you work out and train as a regular part of your routine, you are not nearly up to six hours on a court every day for five days in a row.

Thirty hours of play over five days might not seem like much, but if you compare it to how much time you actually spend playing now, you can see it's quite a bit.

It's a shame for someone to spend the money it takes to stay in a tennis resort for a week, not to mention the cost of transportation, and after the first active day of instruction, practice, and play, be downed by a serious case of foot blisters. Or to find no stamina for the second, third, and fourth days' activities. Usually the people who poop out after the first day come back revived at the end of the week, driven by the idea of its being their last day and wanting to get their money's worth. If you go to a tennis week in an out-of-condition state, you'll never be able to get the maximum benefit from the program, no matter how well it's run.

You have an obligation—to yourself, to the facility where you will be in attendance, to your fellow students, and to the game. You need to be ready to do your best. This means being physically able to perform at your maximum, as well as mentally able to adjust to a new situation and the ardors of thirty or forty hours of tennis in five or six days.

IT'S WHAT YOU MAKE IT

The tennis week can be a rewarding experience. Or it can be second only in disaster potential to an earthquake in New York City.

How well it turns out depends upon your selection of the right place, the right people for your best interest, and your personal preparation for a full immersion effort.

If you decide to go on a tennis week, go ready for bear. Go to learn. But most of all, go to have a good time.

10
How You Play
Is Affected by
What You Play With

"Yeah, I know Bert. He's not a bad player, but he belongs to the racket-of-the-month club."
Jason Morton

"Hugh Sweeney was six feet five inches tall and must have weighed all of a hundred and ten pounds. He was taking medication because he was anemic. It left him a little weak, but he carried on and became a good player. It took work, though.

"The first time we paired off against each other we were still in high school. I beat him the first set playing right-handed, then took the second left-handed just to see if I could do it.

"Hugh had a great personality back then. Still does, but I don't see him much anymore. He was not a winner of major tournaments, but he played all over the world and was always invited back. Because he had style. He dressed in keeping with his conservative personality."

Jason sat back in his chair and watched a doubles match on the indoor court next to the tennis lounge in the University Club. He was smiling to himself over some memory.

Russell, intense as ever, leaned forward, resting his weight on his tanned forearms. Without taking his eyes off the players, he nodded agreement.

"I played him once. First round at Wimbledon. He wasn't bad at all. Something would always seem to break his concentration. He had the shots

139

down right enough. I took the first game of the first set easily, and in the second game I knocked him a great high lob. Sweeney ran under it and took a roundhouse. In his place I think I would have waited for it to bounce, but in any case, he missed. I don't mean topped it or knocked it into the net. I mean he clearly missed the damned ball. I was astonished. There I stood, ready to return the setup I'd given him, and he clean missed. Then it happened. He broke my flow of concentration. Sweeney walked to the net, all six-five of him, moustache bristling, with a wide grin on his face. He motioned me forward. Puzzled, I went over to where he was standing. 'Sa . . . say,' he said half stuttering, 'could you throw up a few more of those for me. Looks like I need the practice.' It was his unique sense of humor and it almost threw me off for the rest of the match. One thing you've got to say about him. He is an original."

Jason took his eyes off the game and studied Russell's face. "He didn't beat you, did he?"

The answer was a bit abrupt. "No. I don't think he beat many seeded players."

"Then how did he manage to travel all over and be invited to tournaments?"

"You said it, Jason. Style. He dressed in keeping with his game."

Jason nodded. "He came close to taking Ted Schroeder one year at the River Oaks Tournament. Back when Ted was a ranked player."

"It was the damned long, white flannel trousers," Russell replied. "He dressed for the game like a pro in the 1920s. I understand there was a picture of him in *Sports Illustrated* from back in the early sixties. Hugh and his long, white flannels. It put you off for a while."

Both men's eyes and minds went back to the game they were watching, but before losing the train of thought, Jason spoke again. "It goes to show you. It does help to dress the part. Even if what you wear is a little unorthodox. If it expresses your personality, it probably helps you play just a little better game."

TENNIS GEAR

The game of tennis has changed since tennis-on-the-lawn was added to the All-England Croquet Club at Wimbledon, England, in 1877. Croquet, in a more difficult version of the contest now played by children in America, had been the main diversion, but it was soon swept aside by the growing ranks of racket-and-ball enthusiasts.

Early rackets were more like paddles with a small area for gut in the center. And the gutta-percha ball, the name derived from the Indian word for rubber, was nothing like we know it today.

There have been a lot of changes down through the years, some for the good and others merely faddish. This has given rise to a variety of equipment. If you approach the subject of tennis gear logically, you can break the necessary accouterments into five categories:

1. Rackets
2. Strings
3. Balls
4. Shoes
5. Clothing

Anything outside this simple outline isn't necessary to play. It might be argued clothes are not essential to the game, but little active, fast tennis is played in nudist camps because the players lack the necessary support for certain parts of their anatomy.

A brief discussion of each item in the five categories will give you a sound base for purchasing the equipment you need to play your best.

Before starting, however, there are a few things to be covered. First, aside from some designed-in features you may or may not be able to use to the utmost advantage, most equipment available today is pretty good. Some is expensive, and therefore gains cachet among certain players, even if it doesn't suit their style of play.

Don't be too swayed by the recommendations of others. With rackets, what works for one person might be a complete bust for you. A relationship with a good pro can be advantageous in selecting equipment, because he or she generally has, or can obtain on a loan basis, the basic items for you to try before you buy. There is no substitute for a trial.

IT'S NOT HOW MUCH YOU PAY, BUT HOW THE EQUIPMENT PLAYS

The most expensive lines may not be the best for you. Don't be lulled into complacency by buying the highest priced racket or special balls. They may be fine values, regardless of price, but they may not fit the way you play.

Also, please, please don't belong to the racket-of-the-month club. You'll end up spending a lot of bucks and play worse tennis than if you'd stuck to a single choice and learned to use it well. As some players believe the mere act of taking lessons, necessarily, without practice or effort, makes them better players, others seem to feel the latest fad-designed racket is a conjurer's wand. Buy one and you automatically make points.

If there were a supreme anything in the game, a device which gave every player an instant edge, everyone would have it. Every pro doesn't own the same racket, play with the same balls, or use the identical brand of shoes.

New equipment can be useful under selected conditions, and it's not a good idea to play with worn-out tackle. But this is not to say you or any other player has a crying need for the latest, most up-to-date golliflodget just because some top pro uses or recommends it.

Some people get a sentimental attachment to their rackets. It borders on the superstitious. Many players believe one is "luckier" than another. Possibly it gives them a boost. Belief, after all, if it's sincere, is a form of concentration. But addiction, a nameless craving which leaves you without any confidence, is misplaced when it comes to equipment. One racket might work better than another on some days. There are some hard, practical, scientific reasons for this phenomenon, which is quite different from a semi-metaphysical belief.

FADS IN TENNIS GEAR

Considerable time has been spent by the leading firms in designing tennis equipment as we know it today. Along the way, there have been mistakes. Ideas which sounded good sometimes did not suit a broad enough spectrum of players, or just plain didn't work, or failed to perform well enough to justify the cost.

Most "breakthroughs," as they have been called in advertising and promotion, were widely acclaimed. Full-page four-color ads, money paid to pros to use the new wonder, stories in the enthusiast magazines; all these and more were called into action for the sole purpose of selling you, getting you to buy the latest weapon. Some of the ideas were sound, and as time passed, they were improved. Others fell by the way.

Fads come and fads go, but good, reliable equipment, manufactured to high standards based on practical design, lingers on. Don't be caught up in the whirlwind of new-for-new's sake. Dance with who brung you. Only change when it has been demonstrated a change will improve your game. To change and stay the same is senseless, not to mention expensive.

THE VALUE OF DEALING WITH A PRO SHOP

A tennis pro shop is hard to beat when it comes to buying tennis equipment. Sporting goods' dealers and department stores carry a good line of merchandise but they sometimes fall down in the area of knowledgeable sales personnel. Questions about the relative stiffness of various racket frames may bring blank looks and little information. Since most rackets sold through regular distribution channels will come prestrung from the factory, you lose the choice of both tension and material. We'll discuss this more later.

Pro shops dealing in tennis equipment, like those handling lines of golfing gear, depend upon a single type of merchandise and the support of enthusiasts to make a living. The people who work in these facilities are usually players who love the game. They know what they sell through first-hand use and can give you valuable information on how to obtain maximum performance from each item.

The pro shop has another advantage over the broader-based retailer. The person responsible for selecting merchandise in the tennis-only facility knows more about the sport and the players than anyone could expect the buyer for the department store or sporting goods establishment usually to know. Superior knowledge keeps low-priced, flashy-junk tackle out of the pro shop inventory.

The tennis store will have a number of price choices. None will be as low as what is available off the rack at the sporting goods store, and some of the items, at the top of the line, will be far higher in price than will be seen in the normal retail facility. But dollar for dollar, at least in a professional's judgment, the rackets, balls, shoes, and clothing on display offer each customer the maximum value.

There are some competently operated tennis departments in the broader-based retail establishments. Outside the major cities and resorts, though, the pro shop is usually a player's best bet.

THE TENNIS RACKET

The tennis racket is a simple-appearing device. If you bent a stick and tied it into place with a web of dried gut or rawhide, you'd have a crude playing instrument similar to some used in ancient ball games and found in certain archaeological digs.

It's a long way from a bent stick, however, to a pressure-formed fiber and graphite instrument designed with tremendous flexibility and energy-storing capacities.

For many years, research on rackets was limited to the techniques and materials used to make wooden laminations. The type of wood, the curing process, the glues and resins utilized to hold the layers together, and even the angle at which the various laminates were joined were questions that drove small scientific teams in manufacturing research centers to make test run after test run. The results from more than thirty years of this endeavor produced a number of exceptional, well-designed, durable wooden rackets which became the standard of the game. All pro players used wood and were happy with it.

Through the years, individuals experimented with the idea of other materials for racket construction, but were unsuccessful in their efforts to make as serviceable a tool as the highly developed wooden standard.

Then came the Wilson T-2000. It was, in a way, a variation of one of the older ideas, used for a while by LaCoste. But it took World War II and the space age to make available the right alloys and metalworking techniques to mass-produce something superior to good wood.

There was considerable argument when the T-2000 was introduced about just how superior it actually was. Some people claimed it would bring about an end to the game as it had been played because it gave mediocre hitters an advantage over their betters. Others denied this, decrying the new material and idea, pooh-poohing the notion it would make a less able player better. But after Billie Jean King dominated Forest Hills and Clark Grader began to murder his opposition, no one argued that in certain hands the revolutionary device could give some players improved performance.

From the first metal units, which were tubular and had the strings suspended inside the frame encircling the striking area, others were developed. The same research facilities which had devoted themselves to the study of wood and glue now turned to modern technology for a close evaluation of other materials. Fiber glass, new metal alloys, graphite, combinations of wood and metal in laminations, and a wide number of resin and plastic combinations were all experimentally tested. Some did well, others better, and still more were rated as poorer than what was available in wood. Breakthroughs were heralded, given a splashy introduction including star-personality endorsements, then offered for sale. The confused player looking for an advantage accepted the technocrats' promise of more power or an easier stroke and bought racket after racket. It was hard to be satisfied with yesterday's darling when new claims were made in the pages of each issue of the nation's tennis magazines.

THE LARGE FACE RACKET

While several firms were developing different materials for making frames, one man, Howard Head, began inquiring into the fundamental shape of the hitting area. To his interest, he discovered there were no existing rules or regulations covering the size of the strung area or the length of the handle. In other words, the dimensions of the racket were "free" or left up to the individual desires of the player.

Naturally, there were constraints. The weight of the racket had to fall within certain bounds or an average hitter wouldn't be able to control his swing. But overall there was complete freedom in design.

The size of the racket face had been arrived at through the years by an unofficial, unspoken, common agreement between players and manufacturers. Some might be an inch or so longer or wider, but the number of square inches of surface was roughly the same.

Head's experimentation indicated several interesting concepts about the size of the striking area. If it could be increased, and the shape changed to provide for some specific lengths of stringing to be used, the end result would be a much, much larger sweet spot. The "sweet spot," for those who might know it by a different name, is the area where maximum ball control is obtainable. It's the "spot" on the face of the racket which meets the ball, helps absorb the forward energy, and transmits the new force to knock the ball back. It feels "sweeter" to make contact with the ball in this area than it does an inch or even a half inch away. A sweet-spot hit gives the best accuracy, the hardest returns, and causes less trauma to a player's arm.

The explanation for this phenomenon is simple enough to grasp, but doggedly difficult to outline in a precise mathematical manner so as to allow engineers to design a "perfect" answer. Theoretically, the sweetest spot is the point in the center of the striking area equidistant from all points on the rim of the racket face—or, said more simply, the exact center of the face of the racket. Since ball contact is made by the strings, and they are elastic, the precise center of the face will be the center of each of the strings passing through this area. This explains the reason behind the sweet spot. Six inches out from its anchor point on the rim of the striking area, the string has more "give." It's more elastic than it is an inch away from its anchor because there is more string to "stretch." A quick demonstration of this effect can be obtained by holding a rubber band between your thumb and first finger. With your other hand, take hold of the band in the middle, leaving an inch between your two points of grip. Stretch the rubber as far as it will go. You'll see it's a couple of inches or so. Then, grip the same rubber band by its two extreme edges and stretch it again. Now it will stretch to more than three times its previous length. The longer the piece of elastic material, the more the stretch or "give."

A racket designed with a face twice as large as a conventional model will give a sweet spot approximately four times as big, if everything else is right.

A tennis racket looks like a solid, rigid device. But at the moment of impact with a ball, there are several induced forces which act in diverse ways. The racket flexes in a number of directions. The handle bends away from the direction of swing. The strings give with the energy of the moving ball, reach their ultimate point of elasticity, then start returning to their normal length. With a tightly strung racket the strings are pushing the ball off the face before the swing is really started. As the strings stretch, enormous forces are placed on their points of anchor. These are transferred in turn to the frame encircling the striking face. In response, this frame twists and tends to fold. Its exact movements at the moment of impact are diverse, and every company keeps its own secret computer profiles of how they believe the series of distortions progress.

Added to all this is the tendency of the racket to torque or twist in your hand. The more you hit outside the sweet spot, the more twisting motion there will be, because the point of impact with the ball is farther from the center. The strings don't give as well, there is more force, and because it is closer to the edge, more twist to your forearm.

Howard Head and his staff came up with a primary innovation, especially for the over-forty player. They designed a striking surface containing less than twice the number of square inches of a conventional racket but with more than four times as large a sweet spot. By precisely calculating the string lengths and correctly placing the anchor points, the idea for the new Prince racket was born. To make it work, they had to attach the face to a handle and frame of very different flexibility. The right amount of give had to be incorporated to prevent "steering" the ball, which occurs when the tension of the strings is too tight or too loose for the stiffness of the total racket. A steered ball is given an untrue direction as it leaves the strings. In other words, it is catapulted off at an angle.

The Prince has done more for the senior player than any other device. It gives better power for less effort and provides the capacity for clean ball control. Several other large face rackets have come onto the market, but based on the experience of the top senior players, none has yet provided the variety and flexibility of a Prince.

Jason was one of the first to appreciate the potential of the new design, employing it with devastating effect at the National Clay Court Championships a few years ago. He was the only topflight entrant with an outsize device, and several other players laughed. After his performance the scoffers bought one for themselves. A year later at the same championship event virtually every top-seeded contestant had one.

Part of the reason was the added power and accuracy. The other part was the relief of a few "sore arm" symptoms including the famous and dreaded tennis elbow. Caused by an inflammation of certain ligaments and the joint of the elbow of the striking arm, this can be a painful and debilitating malady. For years, doctors speculated the cause of this inflamed condition was the torque or twist of the racket at the moment of impact with the ball. The twisting transmits itself down the shaft, through the handle, and into the player's arm. Some is soaked up in the wrist, which is designed as a flexible connection. The leftover force has to be dissipated somehow so it travels up the forearm to the elbow, a one-directional joint. The side movement forces the bones apart, irritates the ligaments, and produces the soreness.

With the Prince racket, several sufferers were cured, or at least given the ability to play again without the pain which previously plagued them.

Others were not helped at all. Although the fact seems curious, its explanation falls within the bounds of common sense. There are players, even winning ones, who don't hit in the sweet spot. In these cases, the larger face creates a worse problem than the conventional-size one. If you constantly make contact outside the boundary of this key area, the ball is striking farther away from the center line (an imaginary locus of points running up the center of the handle, through the shaft, and across the very middle of the face), and this makes more torque, because it allows the ball to strike farther out toward the edge and still be somewhat controlled. It's like a lever. With an ordinary face, you have about six inches on either side of the center. With an oversize face there are eight or more. The additional inches magnify the forces of torque, so the twisting is more defined. It's a magnitude harder.

After the Prince development, a German firm, realizing there were no limitations on either size or style, came up with another innovation. They used a nonsymmetrical system of stringing in which the thickness, and therefore the elasticity, of each string was varied. Called the "spaghetti" racket, it was unbeatable in the hands of a semitalented player who generated spin on a ball. Coupling an oversize face and its accompanying large sweet spot with strings that would give at varying rates, they achieved a striking surface which would induce not only top spin but some sideways rotation into any ball snapping off its strings. The racket wasn't too good in the hands of the hard hitter, because the stringing was, by necessity, rather loose in tension to keep the ball in place for a longer period of time. It was an effective innovation which worked for certain players.

Enough was enough. The regulatory pundits of tennis sat in judgment on the various heresies and found the oversize face all right, if perhaps somewhat unsportsmanlike, and the spaghetti stringing unacceptable. These rulings will define research limits for future designs.

A racket, as we have seen, is a complex piece of engineering skill. Its weight, size, stiffness, flexibility, and tendency to torque are all factors in design. These are compounded by the type and tension of the stringing material used.

Racket Materials

Today, several materials are available for racket bodies. And several sizes of striking faces can be had in almost any combination of glass, wood, metal, or graphite. Which are the best? What are the differences? Which will work best for you?

These are tough questions. The following may prove to be of some help in answering them.

First, price is not a valid criterion for selecting a racket. Many players buy the most expensive, because they like to tell their friends they are playing with an ABC Widget X-11, 2000 Signature model. Since everyone knows it costs over $300, they are supposed to be impressed. A smart player who understands a little about the various characteristics of available rackets might find it strange a light hitter has equipment designed for a person who slams the ball with enormous power.

Rackets are designed for various degrees of stroke force. A hard hitter needs a stiff frame with high-tension stringing. The stiffness and tautness of the strings adds to the force of the stroke. A softer hitting player, using the same setup, would never bend the racket module enough to allow for any give, so would find his shots moving faster but going wild.

Wood Rackets

A first-class wood racket is still a good weapon. It has a built-in flexibility, can take undue strain, and is superb in play. It is also well balanced. Wood has only one drawback. Its natural resiliency results in a certain amount of wear each time the ball is struck. Flexing slowly deteriorates the overall structure. While this is true for other materials as well, none are so reactive as wood, wood laminates, or resin-impregnated woods. Another problem with plain wood is the bulk necessary for strength. A rim width of about three fourths of an inch seems to be the minimum which will maintain sufficient rigidity to hold the strings in proper alignment at the moment of impact. That same bulkiness, though, gives great shock-absorptive properties, and the favorable mass/weight ratio abets this valuable characteristic.

Wood is a good choice on the basis of cost. Usually priced lower than many of the other materials, wooden rackets offer fine value for the money. Part of the price advantage is offset, however, by the need to purchase a press or square framework to lock over the face when the racket is not in use.

The press prevents warpage of the playing face brought about by pressure (never store a wooden racket on end), string tension, and moisture.

Wooden rackets, as mentioned earlier, require more frequent replacement than other types. They "wear out" faster and lose some of the valuable snap. They become lifeless.

String tension is another problem. The life of a wooden racket is directly proportional to the tightness of the strings. Power hitters need tightly strung faces. Wood will take almost any poundage, but for every bit of extra tension you add, you lose some of the wood flexibility.

Wood, then, could be an excellent choice for a light to medium-strong hitter who wants maximum shock control and doesn't mind buying a new racket every few years, or more often, depending upon frequency of play.

There is one final difficulty with wood which only affects its characteristics at refined levels. Since wood itself is not inert, it will, no matter how well sealed by surface coatings of paint or plastic, tend to gain or lose water. This causes imperceptible swelling or shrinkage. The loss will be greater in the areas of highest stress and tension, so in the frame holding the strings, it will be most pronounced. Bear in mind the dimension changes are minor, but will be reflected in string tension and the racket's flexibility. Will you ever be able to notice this? Probably not. But highly skilled players will. They might not be able to say what their problem is for the first few shots, during which time they automatically adjust to the new tension, but it's there. It's an inherent characteristic of the wood itself.

Wood With Metal or Resin Rackets

Thought has gone into correcting this problem and has resulted in the next generation of racket materials, a combination of wood and metal or resin, or all three. More expensive than a wood-only design, this idea seemed good at the time but was largely superseded by the first workable metal units. A wooden frame was given greater stiffness and flexibility by inserting metal or glass support strips into the rim at the point where the shaft joins the striking face. Plastic resin was then injected under pressure into the grain of the base wood, resulting in a plasticized substance with some of the characteristics of both components. A few of these rackets are still around. Although heavier than a pure wood model, they do provide additional stiffness, something a hard hitter will be able to use.

Fiberglass Rackets

Glass fiber, bonded together with one or another of the many plastic-resin formulations, seems, at least initially, to be an excellent choice for racket material. Fiberglass is hard to break, resists impact stress well, and has a snappy, springlike motion which quickly causes it to recover from forces at the moment of impact. It is an inexpensive material, widely available in commercial quantities, and can be worked or molded in simple equipment. Color can be inserted in the final layers of gel or resin, so no painting is required, and if the molds are highly polished, no sanding or surface cleanup is necessary to give the product a good finish.

The tendency of fiberglass to flow, or deform, due to even gentle force applied over a long period of time, was overcome by the use of more exotic resins or the inserting of a metal hoop to bear the tension of the strings.

Good examples of fiberglass rackets play well, but there is some unevenness in their flexibility with temperature changes and a certain roughness or high vibration in the hand, transmitted through the handle at the moment of impact. They don't feel as smooth as wood, which is able to absorb more of the shock and dampen the forces generated by striking the ball. Roughness is enhanced by a lack of consistency from some manufacturers. Resin-impregnated glass fiber does not allow for high-precision production, so there is variance between units produced from the same molds or lay-ups. The small difference is seen in weight, stiffness, flexibility, and a number of other key performance criteria. Even though glass fiber is used in many rackets, and appears to have promise for the future, all, or most all, pure glass designs leave a lot to be desired.

Metal Rackets

There are as many varieties of metal rackets as there are companies to produce them. The differences are more than surface deep. The early units were created from drawn, seamless, steel tubing. Then, as studies continued to improve the existing knowledge in the field, more and more alloys were considered. Space age technology played an important role in the development and selection of metal for racket construction.

Today, available models will, for the most part, outperform wood. And it's here caution is needed. Power, for the over-forty player, isn't the goal. Being able to add velocity to the ball by getting a more responsive hit due to improved racket stiffness or added snap is worthless if it affects accuracy. Metal designs can and will offer you both. But you have to select the one right for you, not the one used by the latest darling of the club or tournament champ. Metal provides an answer to many of the problems associated with wood, and offers almost none of the manufacturing drawbacks encountered in glass fiber.

The tubing used for the frame can be produced to high tolerances. Castings, where necessary, can be worked on proven machinery to offer 0.0001 variations from one to another. This means a greater control of weight and other factors which act on performance, making good metal rackets the most consistent performers available today.

The stiffness of metal is not affected to any large extent by temperature variations normally found in playing tennis, and the material is impervious to water. The alloys have been designed to minimize expansion due to heat or contraction resulting from cold, so the units are stable with string tension held within predictable bounds.

Metal can be formed or drawn which lends flexibility to the design and look of the finished unit. Good surface appearance is possible, and stylists have been able to come up with a variety of color combinations, round and square cross sections, handle shapes, and support designs which are very pleasing to the eye.

Space Age Composites

For a long time, metal seemed to be the outstanding material for racket construction. Then, in a burst of technology, graphite and glass-reinforced graphite, held together with a resin, slipped in. This construction is quite expensive because of material costs and the need for concentrated quality control to maintain a consistent final product. Stiffer than most metal designs, the graphite racket appears to be able to store more energy while in its deformed state, then give some back as the ball leaves the strings. The added zing means a harder hit with a faster return. Some of this is good. Again, in the hands of certain players, it might be an advantage. To others, it could produce no improvement or even give negative results.

No Right or Wrong Racket

As you can see there is no "right" or "wrong" design. What works best for you may not suit another player. Dissatisfaction with a racket usually comes about because it's the wrong design in the right hands. It's a case of using a Rolls-Royce to haul dirt. It will do it, but there is equipment designed to do the job better.

Your professional can help you find the right racket for your game. As you progress, you might need to change, to reflect your new style of play. By all means, try a racket before you buy it. Even though a demonstration model might not be strung to your particular needs, you can get an idea of how well you are going to be able to do before you make a costly mistake.

Over-forty players, regardless of their experience, should consider at least a trial of the new oversize rackets. It may take a set or two to get accustomed to the different feel of the larger hitting area, but it will be well worth it.

The first time Russell and Jason squared off in tournament competition against each other, Jason had a Prince. As Russell put it later, "The damned thing sounded different when it hit the ball. It didn't look awfully fast, but I lost the first set."

The large-size sweet spot offered by the big-faced racket provides even an average player with better control. There is more room for error. If you haven't tried one, go to your pro shop and ask for a demo model. It can make a difference to your game and at the same time may keep you from the agonies of tennis elbow brought on by torque.

THE STRINGS

Next to the racket itself, the strings are the most important equipment in the game today. No matter how good or how expensive a racket you buy, it will not perform unless it is properly strung. And kept that way.

The strings are the only part of the racket which comes in contact with the ball. How they make that contact, absorb the energy, and impart new energy to drive the ball back on its way are important in both power and accuracy.

The material used for strings falls into two broad categories: the gut or natural material, sometimes called catgut, and the nylon or other man-made fibers.

Natural Gut Strings

Gut strings have the reverence and respect of most professional and topflight players. That doesn't mean they all use gut, but almost no one questions the fact gut has more of an elusive quality called feel. Gut strings come in an array of thicknesses, types, and prices. The cost of gut strings has gone up over 100 percent in the last ten years, but then, with inflation being what it is, most everything else has increased in price, too.

Real gut strings are durable, but seem to be constantly affected by the weather. Because they are a natural material, they absorb water and alter their length. As the gut swells, it stretches. This in turn makes the racket become "dead." After being struck, a hard, fast-moving ball goes listlessly back without any accuracy. Even the sound on meeting the ball is dull.

To offset this tendency, so-called all-weather gut has become available. The addition of a varnish or other coating on the outside of the strings provides water resistance, mandatory when playing with damp balls, since the force of the impact on the face of the racket will drive the moisture into the gut strings and quickly give a listless feeling.

Man-Made Fiber Strings

Nylon or other man-made fiber, on the other hand, will not absorb water. Strands of these artifically produced polymers can be made stretchproof, resulting in a material which will allow a skilled worker to string a racket and have it stay in tension for almost the entire life of the strings.

Nylon in particular is being used for this purpose and most of the artificial strings contain some portion of this fiber. Nylon wears well and can be produced as a single filament in a range of thicknesses. It does tend to fatigue or become brittle and break when subjected to impact shock, but it takes a long time and the strands show pronounced surface wear and irregularity before the process becomes serious enough to cause complete failure.

With all these positive factors, the man-made fibers seem to be an answer to the problems of durability. But they have a built-in difficulty. The outside surface of nylon and its cousins is smooth compared to the rough-textured exterior of a gut string. This seems to give nylon less "feel," something which bothers many players.

String research, including methods of texturing the somewhat slick outer face, is going forward. The synthetic strings available today are superior to those you could buy two or three years ago. In another couple of years, who knows? Research might succeed in giving synthetics the unique "pop" sound gut produces when the ball is struck squarely.

In some rackets when ultra-high string tensions are desired, gut will not take the necessary pressure. In these cases, nylon is the only resort. Both Jason and Russell faced this problem with the Prince racket and decided they'd rather have the tighter, power stringing than the traditional extra control provided by gut. It took a revision in their playing styles and some retraining to concentrate more on accuracy, but it gave them the ability to hit harder when they had to and still get excellent shot placement.

Stringing the Racket

String tension is a mystery to some people, including players who have been in the game for years. The higher the tension, the less control an average player will have over the ball. Why all the trend toward tightness then?

Because of the added power any racket gains when the tension is increased by 10 to 20 percent. Without any question, tight stringing will send the ball on its way faster than soft stringing. But the time the ball is in contact with the strings is also less. For most people, this means less control. Those players who depend upon long ball contact to get results from their style need lower tension.

Over-forty players are inclined to set their rackets too tight for utmost control. It's probably a throwback to their earlier playing days, when power tennis was their forte. It's surprising how much more accurately one can hit with a little less tightness across the face of the racket. But it's hard to convince many players to relax their strings even a little bit.

Russell and Jason use tight setups for tournament play. They practice with them every day to be able to control the flight of the ball. If you are a once or twice a week player, the same settings will give you more misery than success.

THE BALL

The ball is the third most important component in the game. In the U.S. we have available a number of brands, packed into sealed tins to protect the internal pressure and assure "freshness."

Unlike the racket, there is an international standard for balls, regulating their rebound or modulus capability, their ability to be compressed, and their weight. Even so, most visiting players from overseas find the American ball to be "light." There are two factors which cause our European friends to feel this way.

The first is the peculiar red clay courts so common on the Continent. These surfaces are first-class in every respect, but if the ball gets a little damp, even from sweaty palms, it will start to pick up surface dirt and get heavier. Here, where we play on hard surfaces, the ball doesn't accumulate the overlay of dust. To the contrary, the outer fuzz surface of the ball is abraded away, making the ball measurably lighter the more it's used. People who maintain tennis courts know the problem of fuzz accumulation and the difficulty of cleanup caused by worn-away ball covering.

Europeans also play more with the so-called pressureless ball. Its hollow core is not under high pressure, so the action comes from special properties of the rubber known as the modulus qualities. They are hard to wear out but lack some of the bounce of a pressure-center ball. They change characteristics as they warm up during play, becoming more lively. Overall, they really are somewhat heavier than the pressure balls used in this country.

The tennis ball as used in America is a wonder of production-line efficiency. A hollow rubber sphere is filled with compressed gas until it is rigid. Then, through several processes, it is given its outer coating of fabric. In addition to improving the aerodynamic capabilities of the ball, the outside surface gives control area for the strings to work on at the moment of impact.

All pressure balls have one drawback. When they hit the racket or the ground, they leak a little of their internal gas. Rubber, while solid, is porous, so after a few hours of play, the internal pressure has been reduced to a point where some of the lively bounce has dissipated. Although there are many devices intended to retard this process or even replace the lost gas to restore the ball, there is no substitute for changing the balls you play with on a regular basis. Designed to be replaceable, they aren't all that expensive.

Don't throw away your old balls. They are still good for practice and can allow you to keep your fresh ones for play. One tip, though. Certain training drills which involve hitting returns into selected spots on the opponent's court should only be done with fresh, live balls to ensure the correct feel and accuracy. It's possible, in some drills, to develop bad habits from playing a dead ball.

TENNIS SHOES

Shoes are next in importance, both from the standpoint of comfort and the ability to get around the court. They are available in retail stores and pro shops. Here again, it's fine to buy them from a large retailer if you know what you want and need, but you should turn to your pro if there is any question.

An example is the difference in sole patterns which have been designed to offer traction on the various playing surfaces. Grass shoes have wavy herringbone ridges to grip on wet, slick surfaces. A smooth-bottomed shoe in these conditions is almost guaranteed to dump you on your butt the first time you make a fast stop or turn.

Grass is a tough surface to play upon, especially when it is the least bit damp. At a Seniors Grass Court Championship in Philadelphia, Jason and Russell learned a new trick. Dick Sorlein, a fine competitor, told them about wearing a pair of socks *over* their shoes. The cloth, which rapidly becomes wet, sticks better than rubber. This unorthodox maneuver gives better footing. After Jason and Russell saw several good players donning outer socks over their shoes, they both did the same. It worked, although Jason said later he wore out two pairs. Russell must be lighter on his toes, because all he complained about was the difficulty in removing the grass stains.

The sole pattern, usually produced by grooves, slices, or molded protrusions, is intended to make a shoe stick better. That's the purpose of the shoe itself. The only contact the player has with the ground is through the shoe soles.

Like a boxer who depends upon a firm planting of both feet before hitting an opponent, so the punch will have power, the tennis player is fully dependent on the contact patch between the bottom of the foot and the surface of the court. That pair of small areas, no larger than three or four square inches, has to provide enough friction to allow for quick starts, sudden turns, off-balance swivels, and last, but far from least, hard swings.

And there, not to become too classical, comes the rub. Literally. It can be a painful thing. While it's easy to design a rubber tread to maintain high levels of friction with a playing surface, it's harder to develop an inner sole, side, and upper to hold the friction gripper onto the bottom of a player's foot. The sole may stop and turn, but your foot tends to slip and slide on top until stopped by the end or sidewall of the shoe itself. This movement jams your toes into the furthest part of the shoe one minute, slams the side of the foot along the inside the next, and then jars the heel back into the rear just for good measure. So the design of the inner sole, toe box, and upper is as crucial as the pattern and composition of the sole.

Sore feet are no joke, especially for the older player who needs to take extra care. Like older runners, players over forty will find leg and lower back problems can stem from improper foot gear, not to mention such ailments as shin splints, usually noticeable by a longitudinal pain up the front of the lower leg at the moment the foot comes into contact with the ground, and compression fractures, which hurt all the time. Both these maladies come from improperly cushioned foot impact on a hard surface. The shoe is the cushion. It makes a difference.

The design of the shoe, then, is vital to good performance. An inherent part of every shoe layout is what is known as "the last." This is the model foot the final product is intended to fit. It may or may not bear much resemblance to your little footsie. You might have a higher instep, a flatter arch, a wider ball, a narrower heel, or any of a series of differences, which is why it's impossible to select one brand for everyone. As in rackets, there is no "best" item, but there are several top lines.

The material used in the uppers of good shoes varies from the traditional canvas fabric to specially tanned leathers. The nylon mesh first seen primarily in running shoes has just begun to make an appearance as well.

Fabric and mesh materials are not as durable as leather, but are usually lighter and in some models can be thrown into a washing machine to maintain a clean appearance. You have to watch this, though, as frequent washing will result in increased wear and sometimes, if the water is too hot, destroy the bond holding the cloth to the rubber bottom.

Several new shoe concepts are now being marketed. Many older players who have tried them swear by the new "double lace" type, with one set of lacing for the area over the toes, and a second set for the part covering the instep, allowing for a more accurate adjustment and better fit. Some users say their feet don't slide around inside as much as with the traditional single lace layout.

The only way for you to discover which shoe is right for your foot and style of game is to try them. Some pro shops have "loners," but they are usually available only in popular sizes. If you are a 12 D or a 4 AAAA, you're out of luck.

Even though shoes are not cheap, the doctor bills the right pair can help you avoid will cost more in the long run. So don't play in a pair of sneakers bought off a bargain sale table in the neighborhood discount house. Spring for something better. If they don't feel right, take them back and try to exchange them for another size, brand, or model. Several national athletic shoe stores and pro shops have liberal policies when it comes to bringing back misfits, as do the better sporting goods and department stores. If the shoes you select don't feel right, return them. They may let you have another pair. You'll never know until you ask.

When you go in to try on new shoes, be sure to lace them up. Then find a hard surface where the sole can grip. How the shoe feels walking on carpet with a one-inch pad under it bears little resemblance to how it will fit when the rubber bottom can dig in and hold. Try a jumping jack or two and skid like a kid sliding on ice, to jam your toes forward. Judge the feel from this, not a walking motion.

Socks are also an important part of shoe comfort. There are good brands which add a little cushion and prevent chafing. When you try on a new shoe, you need to do it in the same kind of sock you'll be wearing during a game. A pair of street hose will give an erroneous feeling, as will just slipping into the right or left shoe and assuming the remaining foot will fare as well. It's not common, but there are plenty of people who need to buy two pairs at the same time, because one foot is a half size smaller and will do better in its proper size.

DRESS UP YOUR GAME

The expression "Clothes make the man" has to be altered for tennis by the inclusion of women. Clothes do affect the way you play.

Self-image is important. A positive self-image is a vital part of developing the winning mental attitudes you need if you are going to succeed in the game.

Clothes help make the woman or man player perform up to her or his maximum, not because they allow free movement, but because they help with the mental process which is a necessary part of every winning game.

Many stores sell tennis-type clothes. Like running, tennis has had an influence on the fashion world, especially in the area of casual or so-called sportswear styles.

Usable, playable, comfortable tennis togs, based on designs which have stood the test of time and made from durable, washable fabrics, are generally only found in pro shops or sporting goods and department stores.

Tennis clothes run from all synthetic, highly stylized, multicolored, polyester, dream garments to simple white cotton with a full English cut.

There are some interesting clothing points, however, which have been learned the hard way.

Tennis clothes wrinkle like any other apparel when packed for a trip. When you are going away for a tennis weekend or for a tournament, it might be a good idea to use a partial synthetic instead of pure cotton because it will look better when you arrive. Many tournament players don't bring more than one outfit. They prefer to buy new clothes on the spot. It's an expensive habit, if the contest is scheduled over a whole week, but some do it because they want to look their best to gain whatever psychological boost they can before the start of each match.

There is definitely a positive effect when the members of a doubles team wear matching gear. It looks more organized. People play better together if they sense a commonality, and dress is a simple one to obtain. Teams in competition can benefit from this effect. Women, who are more clothes and color conscious, have a harder time uniforming themselves than men, but it's not an insurmountable problem.

A word about underwear is needed at this point.

Men have a choice of a number of athletic supporters in a wide variety of styles and sizes. In many cases, the traditional jock strap has been replaced by more modern elastic supportive jockey shorts which look a little like kids' underwear made out of stretch fabric. Almost anything you find comfortable is okay as long as you don't wear your street underwear. Some form of supporter designed for athletic activity is a must.

Women still find cotton for underwear best. Most tennis ensembles seem to lean to a synthetic material for the panty. Some of these breathe enough for comfort and some don't. If you have any problems with chafing, try cotton. It works for almost everybody and reduces abrasion. A sturdy bra is in some ways the opposite number of a man's supporter. There are several "athletic models" on the market, and you may want to inquire about them.

Overall, the rule for tennis clothes must be to wear what you like, as long as you look like a winner! And don't sacrifice design for comfort.

TENNIS ACCESSORIES

Tennis accessories have become so pronounced in number as to almost make a separate industry. Everything from synthetic fabric wrist and brow bands to special training aids to help your swing have become a vital part of the tennis world. Some are great for some people. Others aren't worth the money or the time it would take to use them.

Several classifications of accessories have a valid purpose. Various grip tapes can help people with sweaty hands by making the handle of the racket easier to hold. Others give a tacky high-friction area where your hand doesn't have to work overtime to control the face of the racket.

Sun visors, if you can get used to them, are also satisfactory for some players.

One of the most advertised classes of device is the ball pressurizer. This is quickly followed by the needlelike injection unit to put air back into the center of the ball. It's hard to evaluate the worth of such things. Tennis balls lose pressure and the outside fuzz at about the same time. One with a worn exterior at almost new internal pressure is tough to control.

If you play a couple of times a week, you'll wear out about a dozen balls a month. That's not too terrible an investment for the enjoyment of the game.

The pursuit of tennis accessories can lead you into some rather esoteric worlds. There are branding irons to put your initials on things, designer-originated and star-player-signed sunglasses, and about anything else a creative manufacturer can dream up to make and sell.

What you select is up to you. You don't need any of them, but one item or another might strike your fancy. If so, fine, especially if you gain some advantage or optimism or believe your game is improved.

11
The Tennis Trip

"Nothing will develop camaraderie among a group faster than competing against players of equal caliber from another city, or state, or country."
Jason Morton

It was an unusually clear, bright, sparkling day as the four small rented Ford Escorts turned off the M-1 Motor Freeway north of London. Traffic was light, but on the narrow two-lane asphalt road passing was a problem.

The people in the cars were in no hurry, however. Relaxed, they were enjoying their view of the unfamiliar countryside.

The hour drive from the hotel in the center of the teeming city had been filled with sights uncommon to the Texans' eyes. Huge, and by American standards underpowered, motor lorries loomed over their small cars. Most of what they could see from the freeway was like the view from almost any freeway in any large city, but everything had a foreign flair. Even the signs on the vans looked somehow different.

The four slowly moving automobiles contained sixteen people. Eight couples. They were on their own for a full week of tennis in the land where the game was created. It wasn't a guided tour. They were there in the jolly old countryside as guests of eight English families who shared their enthusiam and matched their interest in the sport.

Since it was late when the plane from Houston finally landed at Heathrow, the group had stayed in a convenient hotel. Then, after a great breakfast, they'd collected their hired cars for the drive to Glastonbury on

Bridge, a Tudor manor where they were to have a welcoming party, meet their hosts, and play their first matches late in the afternoon against a team of Britishers.

Conversation in the four autos was animated. The group was excited and the constant variety of new sights and sounds provided ample topics for ohhing and ahhing.

Finally, after leaving the black asphalt pavement and driving for more miles on a narrow tarmac lane, they were near their destination. On the side of a gentle hill the main house of the mansion could be seen from afar. The small tributary meandering through the green countryside was crossed by a steel and wood bridge. The cars rattled as tires bumped over the uneven plank surface. On the other side, the crunch of white gravel which paved the long driveway announced their arrival.

Twenty people were awaiting them, smiles glued into place. One by one the Texans climbed out of the small autos and, smiling in turn, moved forward, hands extended. In a matter of minutes introductions were completed and the party moved inside the great house.

Jason, who had handled the arrangements from the Houston, Texas, side, was talking with a man he'd never seen before, Cleve Wright, who managed things for the group in England. After the usual "Good flight?" and "When did you get in?" questions they stood before massive double doors. A man identifying himself as the host came forward, holding up his hand for attention. The group of thirty-five people slowly broke off their conversations to focus on him. White-haired, tanned, and attired in a casual blue blazer, he looked more Continental than a Texan's image of an English Lord. But when he spoke, the clipped accent was immediately recognizable.

"Welcome to Glastonbury on Bridge." The words came out sounding like "glas-on-bry-bridge." The crowd was completely quieted. "This is the main hall." The Texans looked around the marble and mahogany space. A giant staircase rolled upward from a small foyer opposite the entrance. Oil paintings adorned the walls and a hand-carved geometric design had been worked in an oak-colored wood across the vast ceiling.

"And this is the main living area." He spoke as he opened the heavy double doors. A servant, properly uniformed, stood by inside the room where a black-and-white costumed maid was visible straightening out slices of ham and chicken spaced on huge silver platters.

"We'd like to welcome you to England and a week of great tennis competition. If any of you are interested, the courts—there are four—are located in the back, just past the brick wall confining the formal garden. After you've had a bite and perhaps a drink, you can walk down and see them. The team you're to play against won't be here until about three, so between now and then enjoy yourselves. Make yourselves at home."

With that, he stepped aside, gesturing with his arms. The crowd followed him into the palatial room. A fireplace dominated one wall and more paintings covered the others. The same ornately carved woodwork seemed to flow across the ceiling twenty feet above their heads.

The servants were busy. Trays with crystal stem glasses of cold bubbling amber champagne were quickly emptied. As the wine took effect the volume of conversation increased. Glass was followed by glass, poured with consummate care from white napkin-wrapped bottles which never seemed to run dry. The meticulously arranged food, a colorful display ranging from orange salmon to shiny black caviar, was attacked with such gusto the staff couldn't keep pace with the demand.

Everyone was talking to everyone else. Over in one corner, near the mantel, two Englishmen stood arm and arm with two of the guys from Texas. Lifting their glasses, they all started to sing, broke off in laughter, then started again. A young woman, about twenty-five, said she was tired of the light stuff and asked the host for a scotch and soda, which, when produced, commenced the serious drinking.

By one-thirty the food was gone and so were the guests. The English hosts were not far behind. Sitting, standing, lying on the floor, the whole contingent was past the point of tipsy and racing hard toward dead drunk. Even though there was nothing left to eat, the servants still continued the champagne and seemed able to mix any drink called for from a small portable bar they had wheeled in. About two, a Texan, with a water glass half full of tequila, was leading a chorus of "Deep in the Heart of Texas." Three of the English who had formed a vocal group were waiting their turn to serenade with "Cats on the Rooftop," a considerably more bawdy pub song.

Two of the most reserved of the group had settled into a pair of leather overstuffed chairs, sipping scotch and talking quietly. A scream, then loud laughter made them turn their attention back to the center of the room, where an Englishwoman, who had been helped up by a man, was swinging gently from the chandelier. As she would sway back and forth. the mighty glass sculpture, made of tier upon stacked tier of tiny bright crystal prisms, gave off a faraway sound of tiny tinkling bells.

At two-thirty, the Lord of the Manor stood. Taking a bell from one of the staff, he struck it loudly. The repeated noise brought quiet to the crowd, that waited for what was to happen next.

"It is now two-thirty." The man spoke slowly, with a cautious, inebriated diction. "At precisely three, the Pembroke team will be here for the match. I suggest our American guests assemble their equipment, take their practice now, and when the Pembroke club arrives they will be able to get in a few minutes while we are setting up the various matches."

With a roar of agreement, the thirty-five people moved in unison to the double doors, out into the hallway, then back to the cars. Many still carried glasses and the serving staff followed, taking more drink orders and dispensing champagne.

Rackets and balls were pulled from the trunks of the rental cars. Then, with each player holding a bag containing shoes and playing clothes, there was a moment of confusion as they sorted themselves out. The brace of dressing rooms down by the courts were more than adequate to hold everyone, so the group split into two laughing contingents. The English, who were not scheduled to play the Americans until the following day at the club St. George's Hill, took seats to watch the games. Possibly they could learn something about their tactics which would be useful.

By ones and twos the Texans migrated from the large cold dressing rooms onto the courts. They began hitting balls back and forth in what must have been the weirdest warm-up session ever witnessed. There were so many different balls in the air at the same time it was impossible for the British onlookers to be certain how many were being returned and how many missed. A woman, after chasing a shot, made contact with her racket, sending the yellow ball straight up into the blue sky. She, following Newton's law of equal and opposite reaction, went straight down on her butt. She got a pretty good bruise and played the rest of the day wearing a pair of pants with two yellow clay circles on them.

The Pembroke players arrived at the very stroke of three as promised. There was a period of introductions, and while the rest of the group went in to change, Jason Morton met with the professional they'd brought along to classify players and set up the matches which would constitute the tournament.

The English pro looked at the Texans, who had returned to their practice, then stared at Jason.

"I see you've sampled the big hall's hospitality." He spoke in a neutral tone, but his moustache was bristling.

Jason looked out over the field of players he was shepherding. "Well, we did have lunch here."

Nothing more was said, but the stocky Englishman was smiling broadly as they paired off their players.

The match was a disaster. Only two of the Texans were sufficiently coordinated to get in one serve out of every three and returning some of the blistering hits put out by the English players was past what anyone could manage more than once or twice in a row.

There's no moral to this story except to say the away-from-home tennis trip can, if it's properly set up and everyone is lucky, offer more than just good tennis competition. It's an opportunity to meet nice people, have a good time, learn something about a strange city or country, and get in a few games which can be high points of your tennis life.

The incident described actually took place on a trip to England not all that long ago. The group was lucky from the standpoint of being able to enjoy a memorable party and a grand holiday in addition to the play. Actually, though, it wasn't all luck because things had been set up right from the start.

THE EXCHANGE TRIP

The basis behind the idea is simple. You and some other players travel from your hometown to another city. How far away doesn't make much difference. It can be across the state or over an ocean. When you arrive, you become the guests of tennis enthusiasts who know the territory. You live in their homes, play in their clubs, yet still have a tourist's excitement and viewpoint.

Then it's time to reciprocate. You become the hosts and hostesses, arranging a full schedule for the same people who opened their doors in hospitality.

Over the past five years, trips to Europe, Mexico, Hawaii, and numerous cities in the United States have been a part of the playing life of a growing number of enthusiasts.

The reason behind the popularity of this event is easy to understand. By traveling as a group there are substantial savings in transportation and side expenses. Accommodations are cared for by the hosts. Sight-seeing is provided and can be enjoyed or ignored. The thrill of living with people in their home country, enjoying the best they have to offer while seeing the more mundane side of their daily lives, is an impressive experience.

SETTING UP A TRIP

How do you go about setting up one of these fantastic events? How do you help to make it a success so it will be done again and again? All this takes work, but it's worth it.

The problem is to allow time to arrange the program. It takes about ninety days to set up a domestic trip and twice that long to plan and execute an overseas venture.

The size of the group is also of prime concern. It's hard to manage more than eight couples. You have to be very careful here, because there are many families with one playing enthusiast and a nonplaying spouse. Ideally, both members should enjoy the game and play regularly. It's okay if only one member of one couple takes part, but if you get too unbalanced you'll find the matches on the other end coming out uneven.

So you've got eight couples. Sixteen people are willing, ready, and financially able to pay the air fare to go to another place, play for four or five days, then, six months later, reciprocate, acting as hosts and having their newly met opposition reside in their homes while they conduct a touring, sight-seeing, and playing schedule.

How do you set it up? A pro can be helpful. It's work, and there is no fee involved, but with a group of about fifteen there will be one or more "free" seats for the "tour guide." This can be the incentive.

A CONTACT ON THE OTHER SIDE

Personal contact is needed on the other end of the journey. In the instance of the English trip, which, by the way, went on to Spain after playing for two days on the Continent, the connection came about in a casual way.

Jason, seeking something different for the members of his club, took on the task of arranging the affair. What he got was a lot of problems, a free trip, and the satisfaction of having broadened everyone's game and friendships.

To the best of his knowledge, he had no acquaintances in England. A man he knew, who belonged to the University Club in Houston, was going to spectate at Wimbledon. Since he was English and a tennis aficionado, Jason asked him to try to make contact with someone on the other side. He did, resulting in a series of letters back and forth. The outcome was the first American-English Challenge and the return English-American matches.

A highlight, aside from the welcoming party, was held at a club called St. George's Hill. Jason arrived to find he was an old friend of the resident professional and his wife, Allen and Jill Mills. The beautiful facility in Surrey, along with the day's action, remains a favorable memory of those who were along for the tournament.

The contact on "the other side" can come through a number of sources. Once, while planning an event for Hawaii, Jason asked the hotel sales staff to act as ambassador. They lined up five different clubs for the group to play, hosted a welcoming party, the first day's competition, and the departure.

Strong organization is needed and enthusiasm can't dwindle after the visit from your side to their courts. Everyone has to be ready to reciprocate. This is why it's best to plan the entire event, both ways, enlisting only those people who are willing to take the responsibility for guests. One general rule seems to hold true. The more people involved, the more fun everyone will have. Using your club as a base, setting up such a match can be a chore or a joy. It all depends how you go about it, and how enthusiastic your fellow members are.

HOW TO FORM A GOOD GROUP

A good place to start is to run an announcement in the club bulletin. It's a simple matter to phrase a brief notice indicating anyone interested in going to London or Paris or Poughkeepsie to play in a tournament and then act as hosts for the same opponents when they visit your city should contact you or the club pro. Next, after you have a number of interested couples' names, you should hold a preliminary meeting. You can tell if there is enough sincere interest on the part of sixteen people to go farther. If not, don't be discouraged. Expand your horizons and run an announcement in other clubs' monthly publications. Eventually, you'll find a team able and willing to go.

In the meeting, which doesn't have to take a long time, you can find when, or about when, each couple is free to travel, which will give you parameters for the dates of the first visitation. After all this is done, it's time to see a professional and serve notice you have a group ready to play in another locale.

The professional might feel too busy to get involved, but usually there will be someone on the staff who will come forward. Free air travel and expenses are sufficient incentive.

The pro will be able, in most cases, to arrange contacts overseas so you can write. In this country, and for other nations as well, there is a pro tennis registry. The United States Professional Tennis Association (USPTA) maintains one, which is up-to-date and accurate.

Overseas contacts might also come through an enterprising travel agent. They will expect the air fare to be booked through their office, but this is of no concern to you as the prices are the same. The airlines pay the agent a commission. In fact, by taking the block of seats through the travel company, use of the airline's VIP lounges, special accommodations on board the plane, sight-seeing packages, and other money-extending programs can be arranged.

Finding Out About Your Friends

As soon as you have your group of eight couples, get each person to fill out an information questionnaire. This is a simple thing, calling for the following information: age, sex, marital status, years married, number, ages, and names of children, family occupations, colleges and universities attended, degrees awarded, hobbies outside tennis, other main interests in life, physical or dietary limitations, religion, and other life-style data, including allergies.

The requested data may sound a little personal, but it doesn't have to be if it's asked for in a sketchy fashion. The purpose of this small census is to assist in matching each couple to one on the other end with some other interests outside the realm of tennis. A stockbroker, doctor, or attorney will quickly find common ground with a like opposite number. The laws and customs of business practice might vary from state to state or country to country, but two business-oriented people will know pretty much what the problems are. Or a woman with a degree in English lit who stays at home looking after her family and two children will most likely have more in common with her counterpart housewife than she would a nuclear physicist.

The information can also prevent misery by pairing off an individual with a severe allergy to cats with a couple who keep ten or twenty. A cat lover might be happy in this situation but the allergic person would be utterly miserable.

Once the data is collected, it should be sent to the people who have agreed to handle the event on the other end. They should reciprocate by providing you with similar information, so your teammates will be forearmed with personal detail about those who will be their hosts.

To Host or Be Hosted

One thing should be emphasized here. It might not be as much fun and could prolong your group's leaving town for six months or so, but it's easier to make the initial contact and set things up if you are willing to act as host for the first round.

You are placed in the position of being able to invite eight couples to come to your city to play. When the professional or the travel agent goes out looking, he has a rather nice offer. A group wants our club to field a team and have a tournament. They'll put you up in their homes for five days, etc. It sheds a different light on who might respond, although it will hold off your departure by several months.

Matching Skill Levels

The next step is to somehow equate the relative skill of each of your team members to the respondents. There are ways to handle this; the simplest is done in two steps.

First, rate each of your players: Championship, A, B, or C. Get the team together and agree on each individual's placement, which should be easy, as everyone knows where he is classed. Then, second, especially if your group is made up of people from more than one club, hold a small tournament. Your professional will help you set it up, matching everyone of equal level skill against each other. The scores will give a fair idea of how each player rates. This will also help zero out any problems caused by interclub differences.

The ratings of your team should be sent to your hosts and you should receive theirs in return. Now you have enough information to be able to make certain there will be good tennis contests. If their side is too filled with championship class hitters and they have no B or C level players, and your team is almost all B or C level, you have a problem. But you've got it while your gang is still home, not five thousand miles away. Negotiation is the only way to correct this situation, but it wouldn't have occurred in the first place if a statement of the level of play of each individual had been transmitted.

Another technique is to make up a qualification list before you start seeking members: two championship doubles teams, four championship singles players from those squads, plus four players each from the A, B, and C levels; or more A and B skilled people and no C's. You can make up the pairing so it fits your friends, then supply it to the opposite side for a match-up. Don't worry if a perfect player-for-player pairing isn't achieved. It will work out fine if there is an approximate agreement of ability. All you are trying to prevent is a gross mismatch.

Finances

Money collection is the next step. The spark plug on your side is going to need cash for minor expenses. Once on the road, there are many things which can be handled as a team, like ground transportation fares, tips, and bills in the airport bar, more conveniently and sometimes less expensively than individually. There are also start-up expenses, involving postage, long-distance telephone calls, etc. These are group obligations, not the pro's or any other person who is putting the deal together. A kitty should be formed early in the organizational stages of the event for this use. It doesn't have to be large, so a small contribution from each participant or participating couple will suffice.

Travel Arrangements

The use of a travel agent was mentioned earlier. There are advantages in using an experienced firm but you have to be careful. Almost all airlines allow a free seat or two with every tour group, for the use of the tour leader or guide. A usual ratio is one free seat for each fourteen or fifteen paid tickets. This can vary enough to include two free seats to Europe for fourteen paid trips.

The potential catch with the travel agent hinges on these "free" seats. Ideally, they would be reserved for the tennis pro who put the trip together. Or, if the planning and work were done by someone else, it's a reward to get free transportation. To many travel agents, the extra "free" seats are revenue. By including such discounts in the overall package, the agent is able to produce a lower per-seat cost than the airlines. As an example, the agent buys fourteen seats, then negotiates for an additional fifteenth, gratis. Instead of filling the freebie with a tour guide, the agent divides fifteen, the number of passengers who could go, free seat included, into the cost of fourteen regular fares. The agency then collects this tariff from the tourists, pays the airlines for the fourteen seats at the regulated rates, and keeps the commission. The extra seat was used to discount the other fourteen. In other words, the agent used the "free" seats as a sales aid. What if the situation existed and the agent only included one-half the value of the fifteen seats as discounts to the other fourteen passengers? They would still get a lower fare than offered by the airlines, albeit only slightly less, and the travel agency would add to their profits by one-half the fare of the regular rate of the fifteenth seat. This is in no way a shady practice, but if you have a use for the extra seat as a payoff for someone's hard work, be sure you discuss it in advance with the agent.

Other Considerations

Money is always a problem when a group gets together. Among eight couples with the same incomes, there will be a wide divergence as to what is "most important" to spend money upon during a trip. Some will opt for the lowest possible transportation rates and the best accommodations on the other end. Others will let both suffer to be able to do more shopping. Still others will go first-class all the way, skimping on nothing because "I didn't come over here to England (or Spain or France) to save money."

Trouble can be avoided by early discussions, the presentation of several alternative programs to the group in the planning stages, and agreement on basic details such as class of transportation, type of lodgings (if you don't stay in someone's home), class of restaurants, etc. It's also good to remember the affair is a group effort. There is not an all-powerful outside body looking after you. Even though you buy your tickets and make reservations for places to stay as a unit, you are very much on your own. Careful planning before leaving, to determine and schedule free time, will be helpful in allowing individual members to budget to suit themselves. Once off the plane, the only group activity which has to take place is tennis. Other than that, each person is on his or her own to move about at will. In reality, however, this would be sad, because good friends always improve any experience.

Another point of agreement which should be reached before leaving is the precise determination of how much group entertaining will be done by both sides during the stay.

Let's assume you decided to be guests, then have your hosts over in the next six months for a rematch. You will stay in their homes during the time you are in their city or country, then they will stay in your quarters when they visit.

Preplanning might indicate you will have a welcoming, group dinner party, done on a progressive basis, to introduce visitors to their hosts. Your group all gathers in one place, then goes from home to home, dining along the way.

Reciprocation requires your team to give the final tournament dinner the night before you leave. Your bunch, through local club memberships or other connections, sets up and pays for everything. The project needs to be determined well in advance of leaving. You might contact your club or a restaurant owner with connections in the other city to make all necessary reservations for the final evening's revelry.

Clothes pose another, lesser problem. Your correspondence should include information on climatic conditions and social prohibitions. The "dress code" side of things isn't so important anymore, but knowing how cold it might get in the late afternoon can be of great value. It's helpful to have some idea of the extent buildings, homes, and cars are air-conditioned in the hotter areas of the world. A lady in an off-the-shoulder dress can almost freeze to death in many Houston, Texas, restaurants during a heat wave in July. Visitors need to be informed before they become victims.

The opening night progressive party, with one host after the other serving a course of the festivities and the evening meal, can be a grand way for each member of your team to see where the others are living. If you do one of these, be sure to plan only light activity for the next day, as the number of big hangovers, regardless of everyone's best intentions, will prevent too much activity too early.

Time is very important on one of these trips. Common courtesy demands you not be a constant burden to your hosts, so it's a fine idea to set up a sight-seeing tour for the second and fourth days of a five-day stay. Arrange for everything, including picking up each member of the party and, ideally, a lunch. Naturally, any of the host entourage who might like to go along are more than welcome, but be sure they know the visitors will be all right on their own.

Tennis is what you came for, so tennis should be the main feature. Time ought to be allowed for on-the-court activity each day. It's a nice idea to rotate hours to cover mornings, afternoons, and early evenings, giving late sleepers as much opportunity for enjoyment as afternoon nappers.

Your predeparture arrangements should include a formalized arrangement for membership in a club. Members of your group ought not to have to hesitate if they want to order a Coke, a beer, or a light lunch. They shouldn't have to turn to their hosts for every need.

When it's your turn to reciprocate, remember the above. Get guest privileges for each visitor at the various clubs you intend to play. Because they are from out of town or from another country, it will present little or no difficulty.

The same common kitty or general fund can be used to cover expenses. The member can find out what costs are at the end of each session and you can settle up when it's convenient.

If you are interested in being the leader of such an event, be forewarned there is work involved. Remember it's impossible to please everyone at the same time. No matter how thorough you might be, you'll find otherwise wonderful people sniping at you over some trivial matter. As long as large matters go right, don't get too concerned when someone voices a minor gripe. They don't mean anything by it, though it can be irritating.

Some individuals who take charge of a group bring trouble to themselves. They become military leaders expecting obedience. Back off. You just happen to be the organizer of a team of friends. If you get a little resistance, keep your temper and remind everyone of your volunteer status. You may have made arrangements but you are hardly responsible for the actions or the shortcomings of the different clubs with which you deal. All will work out in the end, mostly, so if everyone relaxes, plays tennis, sees the sights, and tries to get along with his hosts he'll have a memorable time.

One final word. If you are in charge of the arrangements, don't blame yourself if personality conflicts arise. Try to keep things moving. If all else fails, schedule more tennis and less time as a group, which will bring everyone back to the original purpose of the trip. Playing is fun anywhere. It's doubly so in a strange city or country.

A BRIEF OUTLINE FOR TENNIS TRIP ARRANGEMENTS

1. Find out how much interest your friends, fellow members, and acquaintances have in going where, when. You can manage this through personal contact, an ad in club newsletters, through a pro, or by word of mouth.
2. Locate an opposite number in the city or country your group wishes to visit. Your pro, a travel agent, a hotel, or an airline connection can be helpful here.
3. Work with the opposite number to settle broad details. Will you stay in your hosts' homes or in a hotel? What clubs will you play? Determine if you'll be the visitors first and the hosts second or vice versa.
4. Proceedings have gone far enough to establish a small trip setup fund. See the interested members, or send a postcard, and have them kick into the pot.
5. Call an organizational meeting after the basic details are settled. Review them with the group and obtain definite commitments from those who will participate. Aim for no more than eight couples, no fewer than four.
6. Inform your contact of the latest plans. Put your opposite number to work on providing information on climate, dress, special transportation needs, and anything else which might be specifically desired by a member.
7. Review your team's level of play, and if necessary, hold an inter-team tournament to be certain of their skills as well as the accuracy of their ratings. The tournament is a good idea anyway as it will get everybody together for a meeting.
8. Send your by-this-time friend the levels of your players, so arrangements can be made for equal matches. By this point all basics, such as where your group will stay, departure date, time of return, arrangements for sight-seeing and ground transportation, should be ready to arrange. See a travel agent or an airline

representative directly. Airlines have salespeople who will call on a group to make a proposal.

9. If you've been working with a professional, be sure he or she is in on the complete plan. Settle any details and agree on who pays transportation.

10. Call a meeting of your group to review the program. Get everyone's agreement.

11. Work with a travel agent, your opposite number, or someone who knows the city or country you will visit, to plan a day-by-day itinerary. Send this to your friend on the other end for comment. Remember, your contact has to keep your hosts on the alert and fired up too.

12. Aside from about two hundred little matters, you should be ready by now. The big items have been cared for and your team ought to be able to break free and go. The day before you leave, however, invest in a long-distance phone call to talk directly with your opposite number to be sure everything is set for your visit. It's better to cancel out on your end than arrive to find everyone, including your arrangement maker, down with bad cases of the flu.

13. Enjoy yourself on the trip. Remember, when you return, there is still work to be done.

14. If you were guests, your turn is coming to be hosts. You'll need to maintain your contact to keep details moving and hold enthusiasm. If you were hosts, you'll have the travel arrangements to attend to.

15. Keep your group's spirit up. Have meetings, show pictures and slides, encourage them to write to their opposite numbers with practical suggestions and expressions of appreciation or other appropriate sentiments. If you can maintain your team's fun attitude between matches and visits, you'll find it goes much better when the time finally rolls around.

16. Keep everyone informed on the progress of arrangements. They'll be happier, feel a part of the planning, and thus tend to participate more easily.

17. Remember one thing. You'll be taking part in an intriguing event. The mutual love of the game will help everyone along. If you have fun, you'll have had a successful adventure.

Look at the problems involved realistically, consider the thought that it might be a good idea to try out your logistical skills on a nearby city first. It's easier to make arrangements and find a supporter. In reality, it's about as much work to plan for a tournament in a city a hundred miles away as it is another country a thousand or more miles from your home. The time on the aircraft might be a little different, but the work setting up the plan won't be all that much less. Experience is a good teacher, but even first-timers can succeed. If everyone wants to do it, it can be done. Each participant will come away with an improved attitude and a newfound enjoyment of the game.

12
Doubles Can Be
More Fun

*"Doubles is a marriage, a blending of two games. You don't find two big
hitters or two all around steady players making a great doubles pair. If
you can draw one of each, you've got aces."*

Jason and Russell in conversation

It had been a long match during an unusually hot day for southern California.
The La Jolla sun beat down on the hard surface of the court. In the distance,
heat waves could be seen shimmering off the green roof of the neat club
house.

In the center arena, two doubles teams appeared to be closely
matched.

Big six-foot-four Ed Kauder and his taller teammate Dick Metteer
were playing at the top of their form. They moved well together, signaled one
another easily when one wanted to poach, and had been the surprise of the
tournament by scoring two upset victories over potential winners. Not that
top playing wasn't their usual game. They were both well known for their long
string of victories on the Pacific coast.

The title at stake was the '77 Seniors Hard Court Championship. All
tournament players know the value of momentum. Ed and Dick came into the
final match with a full head of steam. Both men were hot and they knew it.

Jason and Russell realized the damaging effect the loss of the first
set could have on their opponents' morale so determined they could take the
match if they could draw first blood. In effect, their game plan was to play the

entire contest in the early games. If they could take them, they were certain of their victory.

But winning the first set was something else again. A seesaw battle erupted which forced the two teams into a tie breaker. Jason, Metteer, and Russell had all won their serves. Then Kauder, summoning all his considerable skill, took the first two points of his three-point series. Everything rode on the next one or two balls.

The spectators in the stands could almost see the pressure on the carefully lined court. It was a tangible presence throughout the grounds of the club drawing people from other tasks to watch the final moments.

No one took a break. They were down to it. The ninth point would decide the set and eventually the championship.

For a moment, no one seemed eager to play. Both teams had respect for their opponents, but mental toughness made Russell stand out.

"Jason," he said, speaking in a low voice which didn't carry past the service line, "this one is what we came for. We've got to win. We have more experience, we're the number one champs, and we've been in tie breakers before. It's ours if we do what we know how to do."

Jason wiped the sweat from his brow with the short sleeve of his brown knit shirt. He nodded.

Ed Kauder was getting set. Morton took his position. He had to make the return.

He watched the ball as it went up, yellow against the deep blue of the sky. His eyes caught it as it made contact with the face of the racket, and he was moving before his brain had to command his feet. Then he stopped. His concentration showed him the ball would land in the net.

"Fault." The umpire's voice was well modulated and clear. The crowd murmured, fidgeted, then settled down again as Kauder took his stance at the base line.

The pressure on him was terrific. His lightning serve had missed so he had to decide between trying it again or giving Jason a shot at a good return. As he thought it over, he bounced the ball, debating his strategy, looking across at his opponents. They appeared outwardly calm. Neither had taken his receiving stance. They were waiting for him. What he couldn't hear was Russell's whisper. "We can do it. We're the best and now we've got to show it."

Finally, he decided. Seymour and Morton had been playing the net like tigers all afternoon. Most of his points had come from a lack of service return. If he could only muster one more.

He planted his feet firmly. His face was a mask of concentration as he threw the ball up. Then, with a roundhouse swing, he hit it as hard as he could.

Jason again followed the yellow streak up into the still air. The fans in the stands behind the court were a blur as he watched Kauder's stroke. He started to move, then stopped.

The umpire's voice had a finality to it. "Double fault. Set. Morton and Seymour."

Jason turned to Russell, who was coming forward to greet the losers at the net. He was smiling as he spoke. "Well, I won my point."

Both men laughed as they stepped over to the sidelines. Less than an hour later they were champions again.

PRESSURE IN DOUBLES PLAY

Pressure in a top doubles game can be greater than in a singles match because there is the added fear of letting down your partner. In a crucial point, the stress is probably more on the receiver, until the server makes a fault. Then things take another course.

DIFFERENCES BETWEEN SINGLES AND DOUBLES

Doubles is a vastly different game from singles tennis and the differences show themselves in a variety of ways.

There is the necessity of teamwork. You are no longer on your own, responsible only to yourself. Then there is the importance of the serve. In a doubles match, when you serve to your opponents you are hitting the ball over to two people playing on only a little wider court than used in singles. You may be serving to one player, but two people are going to be involved in the return. The receiver will hit it back, but his partner will be moving into a position to put pressure on your side's return, which makes the first serve more important than in singles. You don't need to make a killer hit. You need to get the ball in the service area every time, or you allow the other side to move into a strategic advantage in position. The instant your first serve fails, both your opponents will come in three or four feet closer to the net. They know your second effort will be softer, designed more for accuracy than power. This gives them an edge because they now have less distance to cover than you do in getting to the net. And getting to the net is the heart of a winning doubles technique.

SERVICE ACCURACY IS VITAL

Don't interpret this to mean you don't try to score with your first serve. It just indicates you need to temper the desire for a no-return point with some common sense. If you find you're a little off with your regular barn burner on a given day, don't stick with the powerhouse. Back off enough to restore accuracy. Get the first ball in. If the ball is in play, and you and your partner cooperate, make the strokes you know, remain alert, and stay mentally tough, you'll make fewer mistakes than the other side. In doubles, you will win games.

SUPPORT FROM YOUR TEAMMATE

The person at the net has a big part in supporting a partner's service success. His movement can reduce your concentration and make you nervous. By showing an early tendency to poach, he can cause you to question the placement of your return. The hesitation created in some people is more than enough to lose a few extra points. Your service receiving opponent can cause trouble by deliberately distracting you. More than one player has had his eyes forced off the ball by a sudden shaking of a shiny racket on the other side. Or found the flow of the game temporarily interrupted when the player at the net turned, just an instant before the ball was tossed into the air, to say a couple of words of encouragement to his partner. None of this is quite sportsmanlike, but it goes on regardless.

As server or receiver, in stress situations it's always best to be certain of your shot, which probably means forgoing power for more accuracy to prevent finding yourself in an even worse, more stressful circumstance.

In the match opening this chapter, Ed Kauder probably should have made a lighter serve than normal, to be sure of having the first one in. As he discovered, he only thought there was pressure on the first service. When it missed, he found out how hot things could get.

A FULL HIT HELPS CURE CHOKING

One good technique for releasing tension and combating the tendency to choke is used by many players. They force themselves to hit more fully, stifling the tendency to shorten their swing. It works but you should practice the added fullness before you need it in a game or your accuracy might suffer.

GOOD SERVICE RETURN

Next to getting your first serve in, returning the serve is the second most crucial play.

There is no way to win if you fail to get into the game. Your team is not in the competition until the ball is back over the net. Obviously, the same is true in singles, too, but when you play alone, you don't have someone to help you, and you don't have two people against you.

The techniques for good service return are constant for everyone. You must stare at the ball, fixing all your attention on it so you actually see it leave the strings of your opponent's racket. (The only other time to do this is during a volley.) The ball is going to be coming very fast, so you need all the advance warning you can get to be in place to hit it, ready to step into the stroke, moving your racket into the path of the ball. It's especially true if there is a lot of spin. For some reason, a serve made with a great deal of spin tends to move a player back on the return. The secret of accuracy is to be stepping into the shot, moving your body weight forward through the moment of impact. The third point, which might be considered to be only a half key to the overall success, is to remember to modulate your swing because the ball coming toward you already has a plethora of built-up energy. If you meet it with your normal force, you're almost certain to knock it out of bounds. In the case of having to return a cannonball, you might even have to use only a third or half swing in order to keep it in play.

Many teachers place far too much emphasis on body movement during the crucial moment of impact. Nothing should be exaggerated. Play down all excess or unnecessary motion. Just watch the ball, then start to move forward aggressively a tenth second before you begin your backswing. If you're in motion, you'll be faster in getting where you need to be, so you'll be there sooner.

Another thing to watch for is trying to do too much with your return. The game is going to continue for some time. Play like you understand that fact. Have a series of shots in your mind, then make your return so the opposition will be drawn into the routine you have designed. That's about all you can do, because it's damned rare in doubles when you get the chance to blast the return of service shot past both other players. That's a hard trick in singles where one man has a full twenty-seven feet to guard. In doubles, with each player looking after only eighteen feet, the odds on succeeding with such a move are poor.

Another point to consider is the offensive nature of the serve. The ball is coming to you. You are on the defense. Don't try to be a hero on your return. It usually takes two or even three shots for you to gain the initiative. If you start out right in the first place setting up a shot which almost has to be answered in a predictable fashion, your chance at offensive play will come.

GAME CONTROL

Each person on the court has a certain number of plays in mind. To each of those moves, there is a quick counterdefense. If you can make the string of plays and counterplays follow your lead, you and your partner are in charge of the game.

A sequence might run something like this: The server sends you a hot shot down the center line. You start your move for control by giving back an easy one, chipping across into the alley. The server is almost forced to respond by hitting the ball up, which gives your partner the opportunity to move in for a kill.

Since doubles is made more difficult by having two independent brains on each side of the net, it's also possible to confuse players who haven't spent much time practicing together. Always hit down the middle if there is any question in your mind about where to place your return. Maybe you had a fine response shot planned, but your opponents have shifted court position so now you don't think it's such a good idea. Go down the middle, because there is always the possibility if you get it right between them they'll both say "yours" at the same instant, then stand there looking dull while the ball goes by. It happens even in tournament level play and it's a strong argument for serious doubles partners to spend time together on the court.

COURT POSITIONS TO RECEIVE A SERVE

There have been volumes written about where a doubles pair should take station to receive the service. For the over-forty team, there are a couple of right positions, depending on circumstances.

Normally, you should receive with your partner as close to the net as his or her speed and height will allow. If your teammate is slow, or has limited reach, a position farther back is mandatory. Halfway up is a good trial-and-error starting position, but your judgment, based on past performance, should be followed. If the position doesn't work, and you start losing points, then both of you should stand back, so someone can put up a lob. It's especially true if you have a server against you who comes in quickly with a strong first volley.

There is a shot used almost exclusively in doubles which is a great friend of the older player. It's called, usually, a lob volley. It's worth developing because it tends to hold an opponent in the backcourt, away from the net, while controlling the speed of the game. You'd never see this done in singles, but it's a powerful stroke in a hot doubles game.

The older player must also be aware of the holes left in the court defense by deciding upon certain positions. A younger person with exceptional speed might be able to come over, cut off a shot, scoring with a downward volley. If by some fluke it gets returned, and the score isn't made, quick legs can get back to patch the hole left by the attempt. The over-forty enthusiast will find the ability to do this more than a little dimmed by advancing years. Keep a good court picture in your mind and maintain coverage. You're playing an odds game. If you don't give away points by making mistakes or allowing your opponents to gain an advantage through your lack of position, you'll score more often than by some tricky effort.

KEEP TEAM PLAY IN MIND

Remember, too, you are a part of a two-person team. The gravest error in doubles is to think for yourself alone. This is often reflected in the descriptions of the game made by some players when speaking of the event to their friends. How many times have you heard someone say, "We lost the match, but I never lost my serve." Or worse, "My partner lost service at..." It shows there was little team effort. The statements indicate the person making them wasn't conscious of a supporter who was working to make the opposition nervous, or the teammate who lost service because the partner at the net dropped four easy shots. One inescapable principle of doubles is you win or lose together. If you play alone, you are sure to lose alone each time you come up on a team.

POACHING

A challenging aspect of doubles play is moving from position to poach a quick shot at the ball.

Done properly, this maneuver allows you to catch the other team off guard. Some doubles players never poach. Others, while occasionally indulging, usually play their positions so they can be relied upon to be steadfast. There is a difference between poaching and making an interception. An interception is spontaneous; a poach is a predetermined act.

Poaching was brought to the level of an art form back in the early fifties when Seixas and Trabert teamed as a doubles pair. They had faith in each other's game, so they poached as a matter of course, giving the player with the strongest shot the opportunity. Their deliberate strategy expanded the idea. Soon everyone was trying it, but not with the same sureness and mutual trust.

Fletcher and Newcomb brought the technique into the modern ages by signaling behind their backs before the serve was made. A clenched fist meant the player showing it was going to cross over. An open hand signified they were planted and would stay. Service placement is key to a successful poach. The ball must be placed wide or right down the middle to force a poachable return.

Two seniors, Mayne and Dietzler, constantly poach on each other with almost perfect timing. They make Russell and Jason nervous. It can result in a number of unforced errors. If they are hot, they are really dangerous, but they are using a strong point in their team play to make up for the better work of their opponents. It's not a bad strategy, and it's made them winners against a number of superior teams.

Playing against consistent poachers, though, can give you a new power. It's possible, through watching their play, to instinctively determine when they might be going over or coming across, which allows you to anticipate the action and incorporate it into your game plan.

Poachers can run into trouble because if there is not a close rapport between the players, neither can tell which ball is his. When both stand still and watch it go by, it's an easy point. If you play a poaching game, be sure your partner understands and knows when and where you are going to show up.

Jason sometimes uses the poach early in a game to demonstrate the ability of his team to do it. Once the lesson is taught, neither he nor Russell feel obligated to cross over again during the match. The other side knows the threat is there as a part of an obviously well-organized, clearly signaled effort.

TERRITORIAL IMPERATIVE

Another facet to watch in doubles play is the individual who, rather than poaching, stakes off a certain amount of territory to defend like a stone god. If the ball comes six inches outside of what is arbitrarily declared the promised land, it can go to hell. It's his partner's problem. There is no cure short of death for such idiocy. The people who indulge in it are better off left in their own misery, which is certain to come, because they won't be able to get good people to play with them as teammates.

ANTICIPATION

Another oddity is the individual who will refuse, regardless of the amount of practice, to anticipate the game. To a player who is able to tell what is coming next, it's like being teamed with an ox.

THE WATCHER

The same mentality, but exhibiting different symptoms, is seen in the teammate who hits, then relaxes to watch what happens next. The worst time for this is after an overhead. They run up, hit what they think should be a sure winner, then let down to observe the reaction to their marvelous effort. When the ball comes driving back they are in an oh-my-God scramble to try and return it. Most of the time, they don't manage. If you find yourself teamed with either of these types, or, Lord forbid, you fit this pattern, it's a tough fight. Retraining can be effective, but only after the offender is aware of the terrible tendency. With most people, if they were conscious of it, they wouldn't be doing it in the first place. Here is an instance when a good pro can be of service. Over-forty-year-olds seem to fall into the "wait-and-see" trap more readily than their younger counterparts. Analyze your game to be certain you avoid this particular road to perdition.

THINK AHEAD WITH YOUR PARTNER

Somehow, because of the presence of another person on your side of the net, another tendency which has a negative effect also becomes symptomatic. An individual who is perfectly capable of anticipating rather than reacting when playing alone suddenly may give up the idea of thinking ahead when teamed with an associate. Instead of trying to coordinate moves with his partner, the play is forced into a completely reactive mode. When this happens, it's a sure loss in the making, as there is apparently no way for most people to get hold of themselves again during the game.

   The only cure for such temporary insanity is practice, both alone, trying to think ahead, and with your partner. It's easier to put down the feeling during a "no points" testing session than it is when there is game pressure.

The "no points" practice can be useful in other ways as well. Running an organized scrimmage as in football lets two doubles teams try out new ideas and approaches, work on tactics, smooth their teamwork, and perfect different shot combinations. The pace of one of these sessions is different from a game. Teammates are free to stop play at any time after a point to talk. They can walk through a sequence as they recall it while it is fresh in their minds, discuss each shot played, and consider the response. It can be an enlightening, instructive experience which will improve your cooperative coordination. A good doubles player can team with just about anyone and do well. Contrarily, many strong singles players have trouble with the transition.

COMMUNICATIONS

Cooperation between the two players goes farther than simple signal calling. Doubles teams should not be in constant verbal contact, but each player needs to be aware of the other at all times. A quietly whispered, "I'm going to poach when he serves," is a case where verbal exchanges are needed. A signal is more difficult to use in this situation, especially for the one playing behind the partner in the backcourt. It's a good idea to say something if your service placement is going to be different from your normal routine, so your alter ego can set up a defense pattern to meet a predictable response. If you decide to serve to an opponent with a powerful forehand, to entice him to shoot up the alley, you'd better have passed the word along if this differs from your usual approach. If you don't, your partner has a good possibility of being caught shorthanded by a blasting return.

It's simple logic, but you'd be amazed how many times teams lose because they forget these elementary facts. If doubles players would remember their partners may be great teammates but are not possessed of clairvoyant powers, their game would be more effective.

ROUTINE MOVEMENTS

Careful communication, then, can play a role in the anticipation of your opponents' reaction to your side's last return. Practiced tactics is another aid.

It is possible to go into routines of action that both partners recognize and to which they react in unison. Take two players with strong overheads who have teamed up together. They could easily develop a game plan in which they want their opponents to lob, giving them an opportunity to put it away. By coming to the net behind any hard return or good serve, they encourage the opposition to lob. One player in this sequence stays ready to step back a few feet the instant his partner hits the ball. Likewise, if he is taking the shot, the partner is moving back just after the moment of contact, to protect against the anticipated lob, often returned because the opponent isn't aware of this continual changing of positions and only sees the two pressing the net, which appears to leave an open backcourt. The coordinated movements of the two happen, in this case, without words. They both know their strategy and game plan, realize the need for backcourt cover, so operate accordingly. You might call this precommunication teamwork!

TEAM ANTICIPATION

Good doubles partners must learn to anticipate together. A major difference between the average club player and a tournament winner is an ability to foretell what an opponent is going to do, rather than waiting for it to be done. When two players on a team, either by signals, speaking, practice, or any other means, act on the same thought, they become tough to beat. They are capable of positioning themselves to deliver two people on the attack, or to split their efforts, taking a chance they are right and setting up a deadly return if the planned shot occurs. At the same time they can easily defend themselves from a nasty surprise.

Communications before the game can be effective in gaining close teamwork on the court. In women's doubles, particularly in the over-forty group, many otherwise fine players won't come to the net because they are afraid of a deep lob return. They are leery of their overhead hitting ability, so they dread the lob and don't want to get caught in a position which is liable to draw one from an opponent. An honest discussion of such a limiting problem can save losses by having the partner aware of the shortcoming. (More points could be saved by having more over-forty women learn to make an overhead return against a lob. Half the trick is in anticipating, without any fear, when it's coming.)

Most of the time both club and tournament players give in to the human reaction of hitting a deep lob every time there is a crowd at the net. Making the ball go over people's heads is gratifying. Anticipation gives you time to move back in response, get set, and answer with a power punch overhead or whatever you like. Even though many women find the overhead swing unnatural or binding, it can be learned and the necessary strength developed in a short time. If you fit the above description, go see your pro.

You'll find a new dimension has been added to your game, and you'll murder players who have been lobbing your socks off for years.

REINFORCEMENT

Partners should reinforce one another by each having a strength where the other shows a weakness. One's speed may make up for the other's relative slowness. Many fine doubles teams are composed of individuals with conflicting personalities.

MENTAL TOUGHNESS

Mental toughness in doubles is as important as it is in singles. The ability for two teammates to concentrate, make the extra, extra effort, hold a winning attitude in their minds, and play every ball as if it were the last one they'll ever hit is even more essential than when one person does it in singles.

Mental toughness will allow a team to try innovative tactics without causing it to fall apart. For example, if your side is up against someone with a tiger of a cross-court service return who is causing you to make mistakes, it's good sense to switch serving positions. In this case, you might select the so-called Australian or "I" formation which puts both the server and the partner in the same court, leaving the other court open. After hitting the ball, the server moves in diagonally toward the net to cover the vacant territory. A small amount of the court may be left open for an unimportant length of time, and the person making the service will have to hustle harder to get into the area, but he will be on the move, and thus capable of reacting. The maneuver calls for a greater effort from both players, but can make the other side rush into foolish mistakes. It will also help cut off errors caused by the demon cross-court return.

Mental toughness will let you deal with a confirmed poacher, too. With both partners informed, it's an easy matter to hit a hard shot at the violator, just to show your team knows where everyone is supposed to play, even if his team does not. Being extra ready when this tactic is called upon will give you the ability to pull it off and probably make the poacher think twice before crossing over again.

FLAGRANT DISTRACTIONS

Some doubles teams come close to the end of the meaning of the word "sportsmanship" on receiving a serve. The jumping about and agitated motion on the part of both players has unnerved more than one opponent, resulting in a double fault. If carried too far or done for deliberate distraction, it's against the rules. It can be a hard line to draw since tension relief from movement is a commonly accepted practice.

A mentally tough team mutually supportive of one another can easily block out this problem, the server through concentration on a small area of the court where the ball should go after it's hit, and the other partner by being calm and encouraging.

PRACTICE CONCENTRATION

A good doubles team will manage to apply mental toughness to its practice periods. Usually, in a practice or pregame warm-up, everyone goes out and hits the ball back and forth, which doesn't make too much sense. In doubles you have the opportunity to practice against each other and still strengthen the team effort.

One part of a session might consist of each partner hitting fifty serves, while the teammate tries to return them. Then both players switch off to get the benefit of the fine tuning and endurance produced by putting everything they have into a hundred serves. An hour spent this way is a better investment than sixty minutes of down-the-line volleys and rallies. The receiver can practice, too, by concentrating returns to a specific spot, cross court, down the alley, or by hitting a lob.

Another ten minutes spent in cross-court shots, overhead strokes, and lobs will pay off.

It is interesting that only in the United States does a warm-up become a practice session. In the rest of the world, especially Australia, an hour or so is set aside before the match to get in the practice and the warm-up. Then the on-court hitting before the game can be limited to only a few minutes. Instead of concentrating on getting set, the players are looking closely at their opposition for weaknesses and strengths.

HARMONY

Doubles brings into focus the ability of two players to work in harmony while they use their mutual strengths to build a whole greater than the sum of its parts. A win is more, in many ways, than a victory in singles. It requires good play, but there is an additional element. It takes mental toughness and the ability to communicate with another person under a huge amount of stress.

Responses must be complementary. Each player on the sucessful team has demonstrated an ability to work with a fellow toward a common goal.

MENTAL TOUGHNESS IN TOURNAMENT PLAY

It would be difficult to end this chapter without mentioning an event which occurred during the 1978 Clay Court Over Forty-five National Championships.

Going in as favorites, Russell and Jason had practiced in Houston, then arrived in Florida a couple of days early to work on getting their game as sharp as possible. Russell in particular was anticipating the singles matches, as he was interested in clinching a grand slam by winning all four national titles. Both knew they were in top shape to conquer the doubles event as well.

Then it happened. It started with a slight sore throat, spread to a listless feeling of weariness of the legs, and finally to a full-fledged case of the flu. Russell felt he was getting weak and thought he might begin an "exercise program" for his legs and footwork as soon as the tournament ended. The fever finally came and the game was over.

It was during the semifinals. Playing Stephen Potts and Ted Rogers, two nationally known competitors, Russell and Jason found themselves down in the second set. They had their usual midcourt meeting to rally themselves and take the next points. Jason looked at Russell closely as they talked. "You all right?"

"Hot, but fine." He didn't look too good, but they were in a vicious match so there was no way Russell was going to even let down. A temperature of more than 102° was a problem, but he felt the ice bath he'd taken before the game could handle it.

Jason's service. He analyzed the opposition carefully. They had been going for the ball in a normal fashion, with neither of them showing much tendency to poach. He decided to give them a setup. As he bounced the ball, he spoke in a quiet voice to his tall partner's back.

"I'm going to plant him an easy one on his forehand side. Can you get set to take it?"

The swaying man at the net gave an imperceptible nod of agreement.

Jason took his stance. He was ready. His eyes swept the court. Everyone was in place. He noticed one of the opposition breathing a little hard and looking at Russell with wide eyes. That's odd, he thought. He shouldn't be letting his mind wander. Jason focused his concentration on the familiar movement of the serve. It was time to let his muscular memory take over.

He threw the ball into the air, came up into his stretch, then started to bring his racket through. Out of the corner of his eye, he noticed something was missing, but couldn't check his swing.

The ball met the strings with a solid thunk and leaped toward the opponents, who left their normal positions and were rushing toward the net. One had dropped his racket and was shouting something. Jason's mind was reacting rapidly but the depth of his concentration was such it took a finite second to refocus his attention.

Russell, waiting in a tight crouch, had fainted. Falling forward, he landed on the net, then rolled awkwardly to the ground, unconscious. The fever combined with the exertion of the game had gotten the better of him. When he regained his senses, his first words concerned the possibility of starting play where the game had ended. After being helped to his feet by Jason, they continued the game.

This illustrates how strong the desire to win can be developed in a person's mind and how doubles works at the top levels of senior play. Both men were able to fully communicate, think, anticipate the reactions of their opponents, and force themselves to hold on, while at the same time focusing their minds only on the ball and the shot at hand. It's a prime example of how hard a person can be driven through mental toughness. It also shows the peculiar power tournaments have over the people who play in them.

SUGGESTED DOUBLES DRILLS

Drill Number One: Anticipation

Anticipation can be developed and the sense honed. An ideal situation is to practice against your doubles partner. First, you take the offensive. Agree you are both going to play lobs on your respective shots. When you are set, toss the ball, then go through the movements of making the lob shot. Your partner across the way should watch, trying to see your setup so it can be filed away for later recognition. As soon as the ball leaves your racket, start moving toward the center of the net, but keep your attention fixed on the ball and the return. As soon as you see it hit, start moving toward the ball, beginning before the ball has time to come over onto your side. The motion gives you a base for a change of directions. Try to respond with a lob again, to give your friend the opportunity to study the moves which telegraph the shot. After the point is played, or several exchanges, switch roles and you try to memorize the positions leading to the lob. It's surprising, once you've studied one person's style and seen the signs, how easy it is to spot them in another's game.

Drill Number Two: Serves

Spend about twenty minutes hitting serves to one another. It's time to study the mistakes you might be making in returning them. Serve light or hard, varying the force so the receiver has to change the stroke used to knock it back. When you are serving, concentrate on getting each one into the playing area. If you want to make a few powerful ones, okay, but first and foremost, they have to go in. To make a game of it, each hitter should agree to serve fifty balls. You lose one point for each one your partner returns, two points for every one which fails to get over into the service area, and four points for every double fault. Keeping score will add competition to the practice, help make certain you both are doing your best, and give you a workout.

Finish up by playing at a rapid pace for ten minutes, rallying and volleying diagonally across the net to one another. Then give a final five minutes for lobs and overhead shots. Warn your partner if you intend an odd ball placement, so there will be a continuous flow of activity on the court. It will make both of you move around, providing a good level of physical activity.

Concentrate during these drills. Pay close attention. It's a time, because there is a friend and playing partner on the other side of the net, to see if you can watch the ball off the strings. Bear down mentally. Try to focus your maximum attention on the play. Success here will make it easier to concentrate during a game.

When you are serving, try to place the ball exactly where you feel it should be. Pick a spot a foot square, then lay it in there. Don't worry about hitting the return. It's a practice, remember? Use the time to see if the ball goes where you aim it. Work now will give you points later.

Drill Number Three: Accuracy and Motion

This drill teaches anticipation and stroke accuracy. Player B, alone on one side of the court, hits the ball to A, who is standing deep in the opposite court. A hits back short enough to make B run up in order to volley to C, who stops the ball and returns it to B, who starts the series again. This allows for a breather between plays. A, B, and C rotate their positions every five or six times.

Drill Number Four: Accuracy

After hitting the ball back and forth a few times, B mentally picks an exact spot in the opposite court. B hits to this specific spot and A responds by moving in for the return. The ball goes back and forth a few more times, and B again selects a specific target to try and hit.

13
Mixed Doubles Doesn't Have to Be a Drag

"Mixed doubles is a social meeting, not a tennis game. It can be a real lesson in humility, too, even when you're playing with pros."
Jason Morton

"What I really can't understand is the woman who would never take on a male player she acknowledges is better in a singles match turning aggressive during a mixed doubles game and time after time smashing the ball at him. I guess it's a way of letting off frustrations, but it seems a bit thick."
Russell Seymour

The couple in the far court were obviously tennis enthusiasts. Their once-white Tretorn shoes were stained a permanent yellow-ocher from hours of stamping on clay, the grips of their rackets were worn under an extra overwrapping of sweat-absorbing friction material, and their clothes had the well-used, slightly tatty look that comes to quality material after many washings.

They played well together. So well, in fact, they had their opponents down by more than two games after taking the first set 6–2.

Evenly matched, each was careful to give the other advance warning when a court position change was coming. They called almost every ball which came up the middle. As a team, they were superb. The man combined a strong forehand with a sharp but not vicious overhead. The female partner was agile and came to the net at every opportunity, showing aggressiveness. She hit well and moved even better.

They had played together for years and were known to their friends and fellow players at the club as a hard team to beat. People enjoyed playing them because they were always good sports.

"Oh, tough luck, baby." He spoke softly, smiling, as he watched his

195

partner move into position, to take the ball with a forehand which packed some real power. It failed to clear the top of the net by an inch.

"Damn. Damn. Dammit." She had a look of concerned vexation on her face as she walked over to where the ball lay.

"Come on," he said, still smiling. "We've got 'em. You made a good shot. We all miss some of them."

She took a long look at him, then nodded and smiled, too. "You're right. But I still shouldn't have missed it."

"I shouldn't have missed the overhead either." Together they moved into position to take the serve.

After the game, which they won 6–3, they went home—to different houses and families. His wife is an attorney whose mixed doubles game started at the same club only minutes after his and they drove home as they had come, together in the same car. Her husband, a doctor, had an emergency, so she'd gone to the club for a game and stayed for dinner.

Two courts away, another couple played. These two were married. They were also well known to their fellow members. Each was thought of as a good singles player and a fine partner for doubles. Together, they were known as holy terrors in a mixed match. Not because they were so great but because they were so bad. Their play was excellent, to a point. Then things started to happen. Trailing one set 3–3 in the second game, they faced off to take the serve. It was her turn. The man glared at her as he spoke. "Now, dammit, concentrate. Don't miss this one. We need the point."

She nodded, staring across at the opponent, avoiding his eyes. Her mind was running ahead as she watched the server toss the ball. My God, she thought, what's he going to say if I don't make this one? Tension was evident from the lines in her face.

The ball came fast with little spin. Anticipating, she moved quickly and was on it easily. She returned it with a backhand, right down the middle, where the server, who had only moved partway into the net, caught it. He slammed it back. It was her ball, and she lunged to intercept it. Off balance as she swung, she made solid contact. Her stroke had some snap in it, sending the ball toward the opposition, but it was too low and landed in the net.

"Goddammit, Ethel. That's the second time you've done that." The man spoke in a voice low with anger. The exasperated look on his face clearly showed his disgust.

Her reaction was classic. There was nothing she could say. She'd missed the point but had done her best. Her face started clouding up.

"Look," he continued in the same short tone, "I don't know about you, but I want to win this one. From now on, let me take anything they send us unless it comes directly to you and you're sure you can make it. We can't stand any more stupid mistakes like that last shot."

She wasn't crying, but the tears weren't far behind her sad eyes. Across the net the other couple looked briefly at each other, then busied themselves, apparently interested in the cleanliness of their racket grips and the wear of the strings. They remained so until the conversation from the other side had died down.

What little fun there had been in the game was gone. The rest of the points were played in a strained silence.

MIXED DOUBLES—A SOCIAL GAME

Among the over-forty players, mixed doubles is a popular game. Social tennis at its best, it is seldom played by the younger set. It's the only game many senior enthusiasts truly enjoy.

Some look down on mixed doubles, maintaining it's not tennis, but rather some lesser derivation of the sport. As far as being as tiring, taxing, or difficult as regular doubles or singles, this may be the case. It's still a good test of your tennis ability. And there is an enjoyment in the play which can place demands on even the top professionals.

Women, especially after the age of thirty-five, seem to love mixed doubles. It may be the chance to try themselves against stronger male players, the conviviality of the match, or the enjoyment of team playing without the intensity of sharp competition, but for whatever the reason, it's almost impossible today to plan a tennis weekend or tournament without including ample time for mixed doubles games.

A Basic Tenet

A cardinal rule for getting more fun out of mixed doubles doesn't apply to everyone, but it's true often enough to make it worthwhile.

Don't play with your own wife or husband.

Some do and get away with it. Usually, the couples who succeed in playing together have a common history. They took up the game after they were settled, say in their late thirties, and they are of approximately equal ability, with the man's advantage of greater strength equaled out by the woman's better timing and shot placement. Under these conditions, it's possible for a few husband and wife teams to get along. If you fall into this category, great. Enjoy yourselves. But for most of us, it won't work.

After years of staging tournaments where the mixed doubles pairs would have been better off with a marriage counselor rather than a tennis pro, the problems of married teams are well and all too easily recalled.

Sometimes it's funny to watch. A man teams with a friend's wife, smiles through the whole match, has a good time, and is friendly and solicitous in his remarks. The same guy, the next afternoon, has his wife as a partner. He becomes a raging nut case whose kindest look throughout the game is a dirty scowl.

There are many tasks hard to do inside the family circle—teaching someone to drive, for instance. Somehow, we expect more from our immediate family. We're close to them, accustomed to expressing our true feelings, and they get on our nerves. Why add the stress of an athletic performance to the blend? There's no reason unless, as mentioned above, you're certain you can handle it.

Men Are the Big Problem

Most of the problems in mixed doubles play come from the men. If a man goes into the game with a strong competitive drive expecting not to miss a point, he's certain to be disappointed. The letdown is almost equally as sure to bring about an unnecessary emotional display.

The trick is to enjoy the game, make it into a different type of contest, get something out of it, and come away entertained by a good social outing. It's no small goal to be called a perfect lady or gentleman on the court. If you attain this, you'll be doubly rewarded.

Here are some pointers to let you earn the title.

Smile

Start the game with a smile, then keep the smile on your face all the way through, even when you feel your partner has been bone stupid and must have been born with ten thumbs. This goes for a woman, too, when she is paired with a male player of lesser ability, particularly if the man wants to assume a dominant role on the court. Fireworks can come from a situation such as this one.

Recognize your level of ability, your partner's, and your opponents'. Then play to that level.

Keep the Ball in Play

Concentrate on keeping the ball in play without hitting it through the other team. Don't try to win points. Let the other side lose them. They will, if you keep the rally going long enough.

Encourage, Don't Instruct

Offer encouragement, not instructions, on bad shots. Keep your encouraging remarks brief on good shots, or you'll end up sounding insincere. For instance, if your partner misses an easy forehand, a quick "Tough luck. I thought you had it" is enough. If, after a really good shot, you say any more than a "Great hit," or some such, you'll be in the position of always encouraging everything. So none of it will be heard.

If you are teamed with a player of lesser ability, watch yourself more than ever. You need to be patient, keep smiling, and curtail giving advice. The two of you are in the game to play, not to be coached, so limit your advisory comments to only the points that are causing disastrous mistakes and can be corrected fairly easily. More often than not, though, in the over-forty groups, you'll find your partner is close to your level of skill. When you come up against equally able challengers, you'll have to play as if you were in a straight doubles contest, because you are. Still, watch the advice in these situations. It can be unkindly taken.

Be Attentive

Listen to your partner's ideas on strategy, but bear in mind a great number of players with low skill levels will propose highly complex game plans which, because of the number of convolutions, can never be carried out. If you run across a plotter, listen patiently, then try to get him or her concentrating on the basic two primary points. One: get the first serve in; and two: get the return of serve back over the net. In mixed doubles, you'll win if your side manages to do this consistently.

Court Coverage

There is a tendency among over-forty women to look to their male partners to cover vast amounts of the court. These persons are offset by a like number who are quick to become offended if the male plays in any but his traditional area. It might be a good idea, when playing with a partner for the first time, to settle this point by a brief pregame conversation. It's one more way to keep from getting your nose, or your teammate's, out of joint.

Self-Control

Another point many hard hitters have to watch is the natural act, brought about by the heat of the moment, to knock a top spin forehand through the opposition. Check yourself and the temptation to put them away. Your plan must allow the lesser able players to hold their own. No one wants a game of patty-cake, but there is an underlying base of social contact which precludes hammering the ball into the female opponent.

It's only fair to note, along with the above, it's not always the woman who is the weakest person on the court. With the growing interest in tennis, there are many senior women who can more than cover their territory. Clubs now abound with women who can knock the socks off most men. The mixed doubles match is no place to do it. If you keep faith with the idea of playing to the maximum of the weakest player's ability, you'll have a happier time. Avoid the situation faced by a man who, much to his masculine chagrin, suddenly finds out the woman across the net is better than he is. Losing your service in mixed doubles can be a lesson in humility. It has happened to more than one serious tournament level competitor.

A funny incident in this vein concerned Lew Hoad and Darlene Hard. All during the match Darlene, playing as his partner, kept poaching into Lew's territory. Every time he would start to say something, he'd stop, because she was not only moving across, she was doing it with authority. Each poach she made resulted in a scored point. He remained frustrated, but kept his mouth shut because he wanted to win. As irritating as her steals became, she was effective. Never quarrel with success!

The Woman's Half

Women need some special guidelines because they have half the responsibility for everyone having a good time.

Don't get into long rallies with the man on the other side. If you've played much mixed doubles, you've been in games where the woman opponent insisted on directing every ball to the best player, indulging in lengthy power rally tactics. There are two others on the court who need to be in the game, too, to hold their interest and enthusiasm.

Lob

Use the lob offensively. It's a sharp shot for mixed doubles as it moves people around, keeps them on their toes, and won't kill them if someone gets hit.

Call the Ball

Make quick calls to your partner. A "yours" is always appreciated, even if at times it comes when the shot is damned difficult if not impossible.

Get Your Serve In

Go for getting your first serve in rather than blasting it down someone's throat. Make a deal with yourself. Don't try to knock off the guy's jock until after he tries to beat you out of your bra. If everyone abided by this rule, there would be more fun and fewer accidents.

Play the Court

Be responsible for more than the immediate area in which you are standing. Move it around. Get into the play. Don't look to your male partner to cover most of the court.

Keep Your Cool

Avoid showing facial expressions of disgust, hurt feelings, or anything but fun. You need to remember, as does your male playmate, that winning is important but in mixed doubles it might, at times, be secondary to playing the game. Lastly, don't be nervous. Among over-forty women, there is a tendency to become tense when faced with a mixed doubles match paired with a man with whom she has only played a few times. Check the feeling. Enjoy yourself. If he turns out to be a butt, you'll only have to put up with it for a little while. If he's a nice guy, you'll have a nice time.

MENTAL TOUGHNESS IN MIXED DOUBLES

The lower competitive pressure in mixed doubles makes the game sound like it might be bad news for anyone who is practicing the development of mental toughness and a winning attitude. There is an approach, though, to mixed doubles that can honestly help you learn the necessary mind skills. As a good player, if you go into the game concentrating on control and your soft ball shots, you'll find the contest takes on different meaning. The do-or-die aspect fades and you'll discover you have to hold your mind on the action. Your chances to anticipate which shot is coming next, move into position to receive it or assist your partner, and make precise returns to predetermined spots are greater, because the pace of the play will probably be slower.

Coming out onto the court with an attitude of "I don't want to lose" is a sure way to push yourself into an unenjoyable game. Arriving with a sense of anticipating a social event and the opportunity to concentrate on ball placement will give you a base for a good time.

More experienced players, including many professionals, have learned to make the game challenging by adding a level of finesse. They play for angles and use lobs, help their partners gain a stronger sense of anticipation. They concentrate on everyone's enjoyment of the sport. The advanced player can take the lead in a mixed doubles event, both for his partner and for the other side. It's a bit like dancing. Either the man or the woman can lead, but someone has to or the couple goes nowhere.

DON'T BE AFRAID TO PLAY TO YOUR LEVEL

Another tip for women players centers on a socially ingrained attitude. In our society, especially in the over-forty age group, women sometimes don't wish to appear too dominant in the presence of men. When they get into a mixed match they tend to stay back. Don't do it. Play a mixed doubles game. Go for hard shots. Be dependent upon your partner, not subservient. Even if you make mistakes, it will be better than not trying, because years of experience have proven all one partner can ask of another in any doubles game is not to be lazy. If you give 100 percent of your attention and ability, then you'll end up being a popular choice among enthusiasts.

Mixed doubles has declined as an event in top tournaments. It's a shame. At the club level the game is an important member activity and almost always gets the largest turnouts. A New Year's Eve tournament with an after-game late breakfast and the final sets played as the old year winds down is an especially successful event combining tennis fun with a party atmosphere.

NO LOSS OF EDGE DUE TO MIXED DOUBLES

The tournament players who have a constant need to be ready for competition aren't looking for the fun aspects as much as the win. They appear to feel the mixed game might take off their edge. Except for a few hard chargers who are unable to redirect their thinking, though, this just doesn't seem to be true. The record books show in the late fifties and early sixties the leading players played everything: singles, doubles, mixed doubles, and if they'd had it, solitaire against a backboard. Earlier, stars like Sedgeman, Riggs, Seixas, and others found no difficulty in adjusting their minds to match the contest in which they were entered. Compared to men's singles at this level of play the mixed doubles contest was something of a break in the physical demands placed on the competitors, but it still took total concentration and a mighty effort to bring home a trophy and some cash.

BE COMPETITIVE GENTLY

Parts of this discussion of the fun aspects of mixed doubles might lead you to a false conclusion about the competitive spirit needed to participate. Just remember one thing: It's still better to win than be second best. As long as you keep your drive for winning tempered by an understanding of the relative ability of all participants and harnessed so as not to cause grief to your partner, you'll be all right. No one should go out onto the court intending to do less than his best. Each ball played is important. Every shot hit is worth hitting properly. It's just in mixed doubles the terms "doing your best," "important," and "hitting properly" need to be seen in a different perspective. In this game the ball should be kept in play and points scored by your opponents' mistakes rather than by your spiking them in. Maybe a look at some tactics can help define this better.

Overhead Shots

Most women over thirty-five, unless they are quite active players, have, as was discussed in the previous chapter, a difficult time hitting overheads well. They keep back from the net because they are always wary of a lob. If one of the women in a mixed doubles game falls into this, it's okay to use the weakness, as long as you don't overdo it. If you're playing with someone who has lob phobia (men develop it, too), encourage your partner to try getting to the net anyway. You'll lose a point or so, but if your opponents are sensible people they won't pound you to death. They'll try it once or twice, find out it works, then concentrate on finding something else. You can bet, however, they'll come back to this lack of skill if they get too far behind or need a crucial point, so you need to watch your team to be sure the maneuver is tempered by common sense. Still, the experience of coming to the net and answering a few of those lobs with an overhead will help your teammate and could go a long way toward correcting his deficiency.

Women Players Are Stronger

There are conflicting ideas concerning teamwork and game plans for mixed doubles. Many come from an era in which professionals and writers made the dangerous assumption the man was always the strongest player. This might have been the case before thirty million people took up the game, but it isn't necessarily so today. In the forty-plus category there are countless strong female players. Many enthusiastic women play five or six times a week, practice, and take regular lessons. That much time on the court is almost guaranteed to make them stronger players than their male counterparts who ride a desk chair all week and get out only on Saturday or Sunday. So watch out for any "rules" which fail to reflect our present life-styles.

Watch the Middle

A solid principle of the game is to put strength down the middle. This makes good sense, but when it's interpreted to mean the woman should always play the forehand court it becomes dangerous. In most over-forty couples this will probably be the case. Not always, however. The strongest player, the one with the best forehand, overhead, and backhand return, should be assigned to the ad court, to make those shots that score game points.

Another tested, hard-to-fault rule is to let each player decide the position in which he is most comfortable, then play there. If the two are forthright with one another, this alone can result in a satisfying tennis game.

Serving to the Backhand

An almost sure way of picking up a point in the over-forty league of mixed doubles is to have your team's service to the opposing woman always go to her backhand side. Placement again is the name of this game. Some will be able to return the ball, but more will blow it.

Here, sportsmanship and the unwritten rules of mixed doubles play enter into the tactics decision. The woman on team A finds she is able frequently to score on the opposing woman by getting her first serve into her opponent's backhand area. Should she do it every time it's her service? It will guarantee a win all right, but it will also ensure a low level of popularity among social peers who play the game regularly. Once in a while, fine. On critical points, certainly. But time after tiresome time, never. The idea is to win, but not to show any of the players, your partner or your opponents, how much better you might be than they are. People who indulge themselves in this superiority will, sooner or later, come up against or get set up by a player better than they are. It serves them right. But it can never atone for the number of miserable hours they have given others through a stupid release of their egocentric personalities.

Moving to the Net

Another old-style tactic, which still applies to over-forty couples where the man is the stronger, more aggressive player, is to send the male to the net and allow the female to protect the backcourt area. If it works for your team and everyone is comfortable with it, fine. But it's a good idea to bring the woman forward into the heat of the play now and then, because it will add to her game and hitting ability. A part of the pleasure of the sport is achieving more than you thought you were capable of. Coming out and rising above what you believed your limits to be is bound to give anyone a good feeling. If you are the better player on your side, do what you can to encourage your partner to move into the net. Not on every shot and not so often it produces tension or a strain on your relationship, but with enough frequency to experience the feeling of success. When your partner moves in, do everything you can to support. Gaining a few points through quick volleys at the net can do more good for a player's self-confidence than ten years of praise from a coach.

Be cautious. Don't push too hard. If you see you've started to overstep the bounds, don't back off. Just quit it altogether and have fun.

Cooked carrots are an acquired taste to children. Some will try them and others, no matter what is done, will do everything but throw up if they come near the orange vegetable. It doesn't make sense to make them eat carrots at every meal. Once in a while is enough and probably causes more grief than it's worth if they can't stand them. Coming to the net is the same. Many people just don't want to do it. They lack confidence in their shots or reflexes, possibly have tried it before only to be killed, or simply can't tolerate the thought. You'll be able to tell such a player quickly. If you find yourself allied with someone who can't stand the net, forget about it and seek some other traits to utilize in the game. There's no cause for despair, as the longest you'll have to put up with this player, if his lack of ability bothers you, is not more than an hour or an hour and a half. Any adult can hold together that long!

The Territory Player

One of the areas in mixed doubles where social caution may be discarded is the situation in which your partner mentally fences off nine square feet of the court into a three-by-three-foot box, then takes position in the middle and won't move out past the imaginary boundaries.

Directness may be interpreted as rudeness, but regrettably, some players are too timid to respond to little hints. If a couple of casual tries fail, do your best and remember them the next time you're choosing sides.

You'll find mixed doubles an ideal social game if you go into the match for fun and finesse, both in ball placement and personal relationships. Above all, have a good time.

MIXED DOUBLES DRILLS

This subject should start with a smile. Not too wide, but more than a grin. Now hold it. That's not a bad drill by any means.

Drill Number One: Anticipation

Since anticipation is such a large part of both doubles and mixed doubles a simple practice on this skill will stand you in good stead.

Take one side of the court and have your partner on the other. Knock the ball over after you call its placement. Hit it so it can be returned by a lob, for instance. Watch your partner's form so you can get it down in your memory. Before the swing, move where you anticipate the return to land. It will surprise you how often you get it right.

Watch one thing. After you position yourself for the shot, don't fall back with the ball and hit with your weight going away from the net. Get into position so you step into the shot.

Practice so you get to make a return and then your partner has a chance. Each time, try and guess what the return will be, even though you've tried to set up the proper response, and move into position before the ball is stroked back.

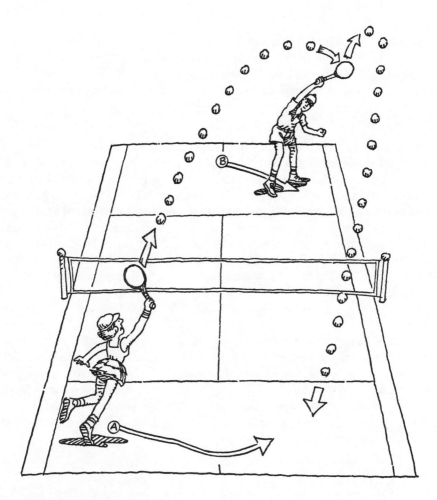

Drill Number Two: Boundaries

This is perfect for the unsure person who stakes a limited territory and won't move out of its boundaries. One way to build the necessary confidence is to practice scrambling.

Start ready in the far backcourt. Have your partner feed you balls by dropping them on the ground and hitting them across at a fast pace. After five or six in quick succession to the deep court where you're playing, the hitter should send you an unexpected short ball to force you to make an approach shot and advance to the net. Then, in equally rapid time, but with no discernible rhythm, you should be given three or four more to make you stand

and volley. The short shot which brings you forward can be given to you on either your forehand or backhand side, depending on where you need the practice. After a repetition of this demanding drill, switch roles. It gives you a break to get your wind back and allows your partner the same practice.

Drill Number Three: Alertness

This one seems too simple but can make you points in mixed doubles.

Take a station about midway in the forehand court. Have your partner feed you a shot. As you return it, concentrate on exactly where you want the ball to land. The shot you make should cause you to move forward, toward the net. While you're still in motion, regain your mental alertness. At the moment your hit touches down, your partner, using a second ball, should give you a high lob, hard enough to be just barely in or out. Watch the ball and try to judge if it will land fair or foul. If you think "in," move toward it calling "in." If you think it's out, move but say "out." Then don't try to return it at all. Just watch it land and see if you were right.

Good judgment on the distance a ball will travel will make you points.

A variation is to try to hit the borderline balls after calling the "in" or "out" to yourself. Sometimes, if the questionable ball is on your strong side and you have some assurance you can make a point from a hard return, it's not too bad an idea to go after it and try to score. If the ball is on your weaker side or you're worried about making an error, it might be better to let it pass. Best of all is your ability to call it while it's in the air, so as not to play one that would have given you a point.

Drill Number Four: Finesse

Finesse shots are the well-honed edge of any doubles game. Mixed doubles competition is the place to practice them.

In practice, your partner can send you setups with ease. Try the stop volley or the drop shot a few times to become accustomed to the force required, then have balls hit over with varying force so you have to judge.

Don't be too fooled by your success. These soft ball techniques are the hardest to learn. They put an edge on your game and to be able to call on them anytime provides a change of pace which will kill your opponent.

Don't forget placement during your practice. Concentrate on making the ball land where you intend it should. It's not good to be able to play these tricks if all you do is set your opponent up for a murderous return.

Drill Number Five: Smoothness

The diagram shows it all. A hits to B, who returns to C, who feeds it to D, who passes it back to A, and the cycle starts again. The object is to practice accuracy and smoothness of movement. By rotating positions without stopping the action, everyone will also get a good workout.

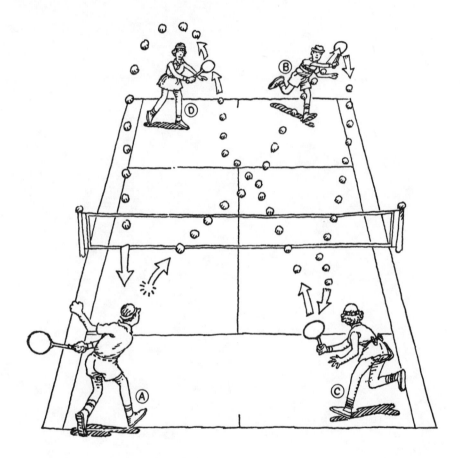

Final Points

After more than fifty combined years of playing and teaching winning tennis, we find a few things stand out.

Most over-forty players need to change their style if they are going to win.

The major changes are not in their strokes or the mechanics but in their mental attitudes toward winning and the game.

A little physical fitness will allow a senior hitter to win more often.

Attention to warming up and warming down is crucial.

Tennis is always fun, but it's more fun when you win. So being competitive is important. And if you're competitive, winning your share is vital.

Knowing where you are in your playing progress will allow you to establish realistic goals, test yourself, and attain them. But only if you are honest with yourself.

A good professional can help you become a more winning player. But no pro can make you a winner. You have to do that for yourself. You have to develop a winning attitude, play winning tennis, and use the wisdom and judgment which is your due, if for no other reason than you've managed to live past forty and are still healthy.

Tennis is fun. When the game becomes a drudge or merely a habit, it has lost its reason for taking up a part of your life.

If you truly enjoy the game, you'll play enthusiastically, no matter what your degree of skill.

If there's a better way to find good companionship, camaraderie, sportsmanship, and the basic fine values we each value as men and women than through participating in the game of tennis, please write and let us know. We're willing to try anything. So far, tennis is tops.